MAUI

MOLOKAI AND LANAI

HOW TO USE THIS GUIDEBOOK

This guidebook is divided into five sections: *An Introduction to Maui, The History of Maui, Maui, Molokai* and *Lanai.*

The first two sections comprise essays, designed to provide you with facts on the area.

In the next three sections, we explore Maui, Molokai and Lanai, with a detailed geographical breakdown of the area. Each section contains descriptions of the various places and points of interest, followed by a subsection entitled *Practical Information.* The *Practical Information* is designed to provide you with a ready reference to accommodations, restaurants, places of interest, beaches, seasonal events, recreation, tours, etc., with hours, prices, addresses and phone numbers.

A quick and easy way into this book is the *Index* at the end.

California Series

The Complete Gold Country Guidebook
The Complete Lake Tahoe Guidebook
The Complete Monterey Peninsula Guidebook
The Complete San Diego Guidebook
The Complete Wine Country Guidebook
Vacation Towns of California

Hawaii Series

The Complete Kauai Guidebook
The Complete Maui Guidebook
The Complete Oahu Guidebook
The Complete Big Island of Hawaii Guidebook

Mexico Series

The Complete Baja California Guidebook
The Complete Yucatan Peninsula Guidebook

Caribbean Series

The Complete Virgin Islands Guidebook
The Complete Jamaica Guidebook
The Complete Puerto Rico Guidebook

Indian Chief Travel Guides are available from your local bookstore or Indian Chief Publishing House, P.O. Box 1814, Davis, CA 95617.

The Complete
MAUI
MOLOKAI AND LANAI
Guidebook

Published by Indian Chief Publishing House
Davis, California

Text and Research: **DAVID J. RUSS**
Editor: **B. SANGWAN**
Photographs: **David Russ, Jeri Kalahele,
    Patrick McFeeley**
Cover Art and Maps: **B. Sangwan**

Copyright © 1995 Indian Chief Publishing House

All rights reserved. No maps, illustrations, photographs,
cover art, text, or other part of this book may be reproduced
without written permission of the Publisher. For inquiries
address Indian Chief Publishing House, P.O. Box 1814, Davis,
CA 95617.

ISBN 0-916841-51-0

Printed in the U.S.A.

CONTENTS

HAWAIIAN ISLANDS

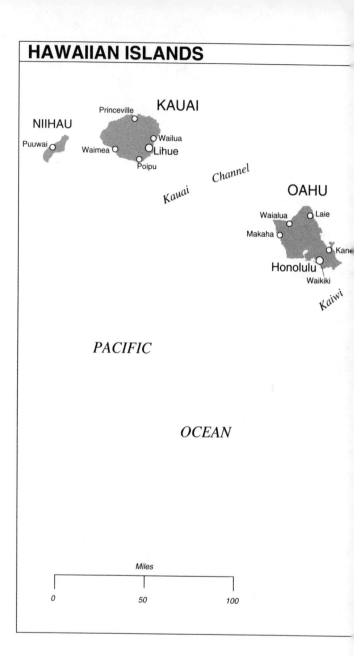

KAUAI

NIIHAU

Princeville

Puuwai

Waimea   Wailua
         Lihue
         Poipu

Kauai   Channel

OAHU

Waialua   Laie
Makaha
              Kane
Honolulu
     Waikiki
          Kaiwi

PACIFIC

OCEAN

Miles

0   50   100

MAUI, MOLOKAI AND LANAI

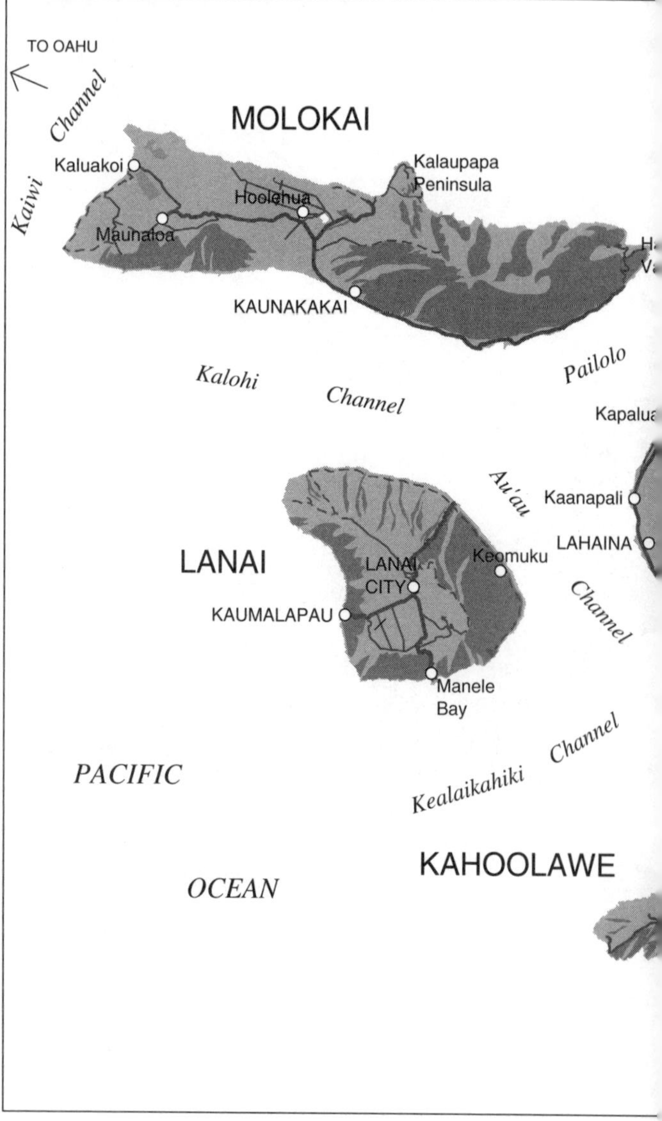

TO OAHU

Kaiwi *Channel*

MOLOKAI

Kaluakoi

Hoolehua

Maunaloa

Kalaupapa
Peninsula

KAUNAKAKAI

H.
V.

Kalohi *Channel*

Pailolo

Kapalua

Au'au

Kaanapali

LAHAINA

LANAI

LANAI
CITY

Keomuku

KAUMALAPAU

Channel

Manele
Bay

Kealaikahiki *Channel*

PACIFIC

OCEAN

KAHOOLAWE

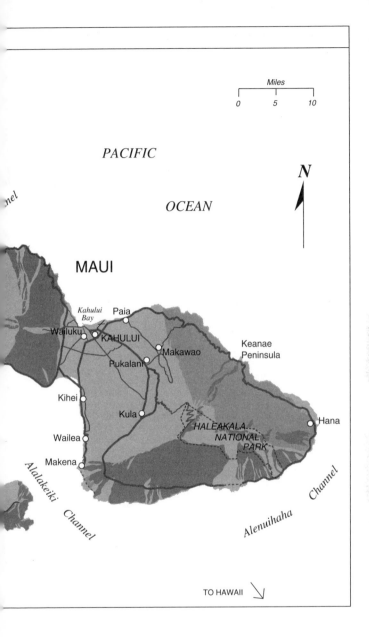

AN INTRODUCTION TO MAUI

"No Ka Oi"

Maui is *no ka oi* — simply translated, "the best!" It has some of Hawaii's best beaches — nearly 42 miles of them — the best resorts — Ka'anapali, Kapalua, Napili and Wailea — the best golf courses, and, indeed, the best, near-perfect weather.

Maui is also Hawaii's "Valley Isle," lying largely between two volcanoes — the extinct Pu'u Kukui and the spectacular, 10,023-foot Haleakala — comprising two distinct land masses, West Maui and East Maui, joined together by a low, central valley. West Maui, of course, has the resorts, tourist meccas, no less, and the historic town of Lahaina; and East Maui, the twin cities of Kahului-Wailuku — the commercial hub of the island — and the sunny southwest coast, the lush, fertile Upcountry, and the fabled "Road to Hana" — one of the most scenic drives in Hawaii.

Maui is the second largest of the Hawaiian islands, encompassing some 729 square miles, with a population of around 85,000. It is situated approximately 35 miles northwest of the Big Island of Hawaii, with Molokai and Lanai to its north and west, respectively, each some 9 miles distant. Oahu lies 75 miles to the northwest of Maui.

Nearly 2.5 million tourists visit Maui each year, and most come back a second time. There are approximately 13,000 hotel rooms and condominium accommodations, more than 200 restaurants, and a wealth of recreational opportunities — for swimming, snorkeling, scuba diving, surfing, windsurfing, sailing, boating, beachcombing, whale watching (in season), fishing, hiking, horseback riding, protea farm touring, wine tasting — Maui has Hawaii's only winery — golf, tennis, and more. Maui also boasts — on its southwest coast — more than 320 days of sunshine a year.

Indeed, Maui is Hawaii's most popular, near-perfect destination resort. It is, in Hawaiian, "no ka oi!"

THE HISTORY OF MAUI

Maui began forming nearly 5 million years ago — the result of a series of eruptions on the ocean floor that created two adjacent, shielded volcanoes, which, with the accumulation of molten lava over a period of time, finally emerged as Pu'u Kukui and Mount Haleakala, some 5,788 feet and 10,023 feet above sea level, respectively, with a low, central isthmus between them, joining the two land masses. Then, approximately a million years ago, Pu'u Kukui became extinct, and Mount Haleakala, dormant, and in the following years, rivers, streams, ocean waves and the wind sculpted and shaped the island, with its valleys, canyons, cliffs and mountains.

Legend, however, endures that it was Hawaiian demigod Maui who fished out the island of Maui — as well as the other Hawaiian islands — from the sea, when his fish-hook became caught at the bottom of the ocean. Demigod Maui also, we are told, forced the sun to slow its passage over Hawaii — when he lassoed the sun's rays from atop Mount Haleakala, the "House of the Sun" — in order that the islands may enjoy longer days of sunshine.

Maui's earliest inhabitants were the Marquesans, a Polynesian people who journeyed to Maui from the Marquesas and Society islands between 500 A.D. and 750 A.D., followed some years later, around 1000 A.D., by the Tahitians. The Marquesans, who journeyed to Hawaii in large outrigger canoes, navigating by the stars as they traveled across several thousand miles of open ocean, introduced to Maui and the other Hawaiian islands the first domestic animals, plants and fruit; and the Tahitians, for their part, brought with them their religion, their gods and goddesses, notable among them — Kane, the god of all living creatures; Ku, god of war; Pele, goddess of fire; Kaneloa, the god of the land of the departed spirits; and Lono, god of harvest and peace. The Tahitians also introduced to the islands the *kapu* system, a strict social order that affected all aspects of life, and became the core of ancient Hawaiian culture.

The first white man to sight Maui was Captain James Cook, a British explorer in search of a northwest passage from the Pacific Ocean to the Atlantic Ocean. He first sighted Maui in 1778, during his second expedition to the Pacific and the Hawaiian islands, but did not land on the island. In the following years, others followed, notably French nobleman and navigator Compte de la Perouse, and Captain George Vancouver, another British explorer. La Perouse landed on Maui, at La Perouse Bay, near the southern end of the island, in 1786, and became the first European to land on the island; and Vancouver arrived in 1792, landing at Kihei, on the southwest coast of the island, then returned the following year, in 1793, bringing with him live cattle and root vegetables, which he first introduced to Maui. These early Europeans, however, also brought with them to Maui and the other Hawaiian islands the white man's disease. The Hawaiians, of course, had little or no resistance to Western diseases, and over a period of some 100 years following Cook's first contact with the islands, nearly 80% of the indigenous Hawaiian population was wiped out.

The mid and late 1700s also ushered in Hawaii's era of monarchy. Kamehameha I — or Kamehameha the Great — was born in the late 1750s, and by 1791 he had gained control of the island of Hawaii, and in 1794, following the death of King Kahekili of Maui, he conquered Maui as well as the nearby islands of Lanai and Molokai. The following year, in 1795, in his bid to bring all the Hawaiian islands under his rule, Kamehameha also conquered Oahu; and a few years later, in 1810, he extended his dominion, through diplomacy, to include Kauai. Subsequently, Kamehameha the Great, the king of all the Hawaiian islands, established his capital in Lahaina, on Maui's west coast, and there built his "Brick Palace," one of the first Western structures to be erected on the island. In 1843, however, the capital of the Hawaiian islands shifted, from Lahaina to Honolulu, on the island of Oahu.

The year 1819 witnessed the arrival of the first American and British whalers in Maui, giving birth to the island's early whaling industry. Lahaina, of course, became an important whaling port, and for the next half century, it remained one of the rowdiest, most boisterous towns in the islands, filled with whorehouses, saloons and gambling dens, overrun by lawless whalers. In 1846, at the height of the whaling activity, more than 400 whaling ships docked in the Lahaina Harbor, but, by the early 1870s, with the decline of whaling, Lahaina's whaling era had drawn to a close.

In 1823, too, the first missionaries arrived in Maui, at Lahaina. Among the earliest and most notable, of course, were William Richards, Ephraim Spaulding and Dwight Baldwin. The missionaries, over the years, established missions, churches and schools, with much of the activity centered in Lahaina, where they built the Old Fort in 1832 to deter the rowdy whalers, and the Lahainaluna Seminary — notably the oldest educational institution west of the

Rocky Mountains, established in 1831, and which also housed one of the first printing presses in the West, the Hale Pai, on which the first Hawaiian-language newspaper was printed, in 1834. The missionaries were also the first to develop the written Hawaiian language, comprising 12 alphabets — 5 vowels and 7 consonants — and translate the Bible into Hawaiian. Queen Ka'ahumanu, the favorite wife of Kamehameha I, of course, became one of the earliest and most important converts to Christianity, in 1824.

The early 1800s also brought to prominence David Malo, acknowledged as Hawaii's first scholar. Malo was one of the earliest graduates of Lahainaluna, who, wary of Hawaii's disappearing culture, wrote the definitive history of the Hawaiian people and their culture, *Hawaiian Antiquities*, in which he detailed the origins of the Hawaiian people, and described life under the ancient *kapu* system, as well Hawaiian culture and traditions. In 1847, Malo became a minister at the Kikolani Church, where he preached until his death in 1853.

The late 1800s witnessed the birth of Hawaii's sugar industry, followed, in the 1920s, by the pineapple industry. Large sugarcane and pineapple plantations were developed, mostly by descendants of the early missionaries; businessmen Henry Baldwin and Samuel Alexander, for instance, founded Maui's sugar dynasty when they joined forces to form the Alexander & Baldwin Company, which remains today the largest private landholder as well as the largest employer on Maui. Alexander & Baldwin also became charter members of Hawaii's Big Five — the islands' five largest corporations that controlled Hawaii's economy and politics for more than a half century.

The late 1800s and early 1900s also brought to the Hawaiian islands waves of immigrants — mostly Chinese, Japanese, Filipino, Portugese and other Europeans — drawn to Hawaii's growing sugar and pineapple industries. The numbers of these new immigrants, of course, over time, turned Hawaii's indigenous population into a minority. On Maui, in fact, pure-blooded, native Hawaiians now comprise only 15% of the population, and on Lanai, just 10%.

In the late 1800s also, after the death of Kamehameha V, Hawaiian monarchy fell into disarray, and the custom of electing a king was established. At about this time, too, with the growth of Hawaii's sugar industry, American interests on the island increased. In 1892, upon the start of open rebellion, the *U.S.S. Boston* landed on the island of Oahu an armed force to protect American interests; and a year later, in 1893, the more or less bloodless revolution brought to power, at the head of a provisional government, Sanford B. Dole. The following year, Hawaii was declared a republic by the Hawaiian legislature, and on June 14, 1900, Hawaii was annexed, under the Organic Act, by the United States, and a territorial form of government established.

In 1902, Prince Jonah Kuhio Kalanianaole, born of royal parentage, and the last heir to the throne, became the first Hawaiian delegate elected to the U.S. Congress. Kuhio led the Hawaiian congressional delegation for the next two decades, and despite not having an official vote in the legislature — as Hawaii was only a territory of the United States at the time — he forged important legislation for the betterment of Hawaii and its people, including the landmark Hawaiian Homesteads Act of 1910 and the Hawaiian Homes Commission Act of 1921, wherby public lands were made available to native Hawaiians for homesteading. He also obtained funding for such important projects as the Kahului Harbor, Maui's only deep-water port, and Pearl Harbor at Honolulu; and in 1919 and 1920, he introduced the first two successive bills for statehood for Hawaii in the House of Representatives. In 1922, however, Kuhio died, at the age of 50.

On August 21, 1959, Hawaii finally gained statehood, becoming the 50th state of the nation — the "Aloha State." That same year, the first commercial jet, a Boeing 707, landed in the islands, at Honolulu, greatly reducing travel time from the continental U.S. to Hawaii, to under $4\frac{1}{2}$ hours. This, effectively, signalled the beginning of tourism in Hawaii.

In the following decade, Hawaii's tourist era began in earnest. On the island of Maui, in the 1960s, Ka'anapali Beach began to develop into a premier resort, beginning with the construction of the Royal Lahaina Hotel in December, 1962, and the Sheraton Maui in 1963. Also in the 1960s, the Lahaina Historical Foundation began an ambitious project to restore the historic whaling port of Lahaina — now a tourist mecca of sorts — to its former glory. In the 1970s, the Alexander & Baldwin Company developed the exclusive Kapalua Resort on Kapalua Bay, in West Maui; and on the southwest coast of the island, the first luxury hotels at resort at Wailea were constructed. In 1980, of course, the Stouffer Group of Hotels acquired the Hotel Hana and transformed it into a lavish beachfront hotel, and Chris Hemmeter, Hawaii's most famous developer, opened to the public the multi-million-dollar Hyatt Regency. In the 1980s, too, yet more resort hotels sprang up on the island's west and southwest coasts, including the Maui Marriott, Maui Prince Hotel, and, the grandest of all, the $155-million Westin Maui.

In the mid-1970s, too, Maui's business leaders began promoting their island as a separate tourist destination — apart from the other Hawaiian islands — and quickly developed it into one of Hawaii's foremost tourist meccas. Championship golf courses were developed at the resort, to lure world-class tournaments; a commuter airport was built at Kapalua, in West Mauai, the island's primary tourist area; and condominium complexes sprang up all along the west coast of the island — notably at Napili, Honokowai and Kihei — most with an object to drawing the upscale visitor. The island now attracts nearly 2.5 million visitors each year — second only to Oahu

The latter years have also witnessed the creation and preservation of a series of state parks and sanctuaries. In 1969, for instance, the 44-square-mile Haleakala National Park, which was originally established in 1916, added to its acreage the ancient Kipahulu Valley; in 1971, the Makena Beach State Park was created; in 1977, the Molokini Marine Reserve was established just off the coast of Maui, as a sanctuary for endangered seabirds; and in 1978 and 1979, respectively, the Waianapanapa and Iao Valley state parks were set aside for public use. Also in 1979, the Ahihi-Kinau Natural Area Reserve, encompassing 2,045 acre, including an 807-acre undersea ecological reserve, was established on the site of the most recent lava flow on the island, which occurred in 1790.

Maui is now positioned as a premier destination resort, with an abundance of excellent hotel and condominium accommodations and restaurants and other visitor facilities, and a wealth of recreational opportunities, including swimming, snorkeling, scuba diving, surfing, windsurfing, sailing, fishing, hiking, camping, horseback riding, beachcombing, helicopter touring, tennis, golf, and more.

MAUI

"The Valley Isle"

Maui is Hawaii's "Valley Isle." It lies largely between two volcanoes — the extinct, 5,788-foot Pu'u Kukui in the northwest and the domineering, 10,023-foot Haleakala in the southeast — comprising, quite naturally, two distinct land masses, West Maui and East Maui, joined together by a low, central isthmus. West Maui, of course, has the beaches and resorts — Ka'anapali, Kapalua, Napili — and the tourist-alluring, historic town of Lahaina; while East Maui, the larger of the two sections, has in it the commercial hub of the island — the twin cities of Kahului and Wailuku — and the fertile Upcountry and breathtaking "Road to Hana," the latter dotted with scores of picturesque waterfalls and lush valleys fanning out inland.

Maui comprises approximately 729 square miles — the second largest of the Hawaiian islands — with a variety of terrain and things to see and do. For touring purposes, however, it can be divided into five broad sections: West Maui, which includes Lahaina, Ka'anapali, Napili and Kapalua, and the rugged north coast of the island; Central Maui, which primarily has in it the cities of Kahului and Wailuku; the Southwest Coast, from Kihei south to Wailea and Makena; Upcountry, lying largely on the slopes of Haleakala, and which has in it the Haleakala National Park and the rural towns of Makawao and Kula; and the Road to Hana, which takes in the east and southeast coast of the island, including the towns of Paia and Hana.

Maui itself is situated some 35 miles northwest of the Big Island of Hawaii, with Molokai and Lanai just to its north and west, respectively; from Oahu, it is roughly 75 miles distant, southeastward. The island, of course, can be reached by ferry or commuter plane from both Molokai and Lanai, and on inter-island flights from Honolulu, Oahu, and Kona and Hilo on the Big Island. Maui's two airports are located in Kahului and Kapalua, respectively.

WEST MAUI

Lahaina

A good place to begin your tour of West Maui — and, indeed, Maui — we might suggest, is Lahaina, a colorful little town, situated on the West Maui Coast, just off Honoapi'ilani Highway (30), some 4 miles south of Ka'anapali Beach Resort. Lahaina, of course, is a tourist mecca of sorts, filled with restaurants, shops and art galleries — of which there is a disproportionately large number in Lahaina! It is also, we might add, an historic town, which, during the early part of the 19th century, was the Royal Capital of Hawaii, from where King Kamehameha I — Kamehameha the Great — ruled all the islands. In the early and mid-1800s, too, Lahaina became an important whaling port, overrun by lawless whalers, and a few years later, beginning in 1823, with the arrival of the first missionaries on the island — mostly from New England — the town became prominent as a center for missionary activity. Relics from the missionary and whaling eras can still be seen here.

Lahaina's town center is of course on Front Street — near the waterfront — between Shaw Street and Lahainaluna Road, where much of the visitor activity is centered and where most of the town's souvenir and T-shirt shops and art galleries are concentrated. Several of the town's most notable points of interest, too, are easily accessible from here. Just at the corner of Front and Hotel streets, for instance, you can search out the age-old Banyan Tree, quite possibly one of the town's foremost tourist attractions. The tree is indeed quite spectacular, claimed to be the largest tree of its kind on the islands, covering almost an acre of land, with its branches extending nearly 50 yards, supported by aerial roots, which grow downward into the ground to support the tree. The Banyan Tree was originally planted in 1873, by Lahaina Sheriff W.O. Smith, to commemorate the 50th anniversary of the arrival of the missionaries in Lahaina.

Nearby, too, on the harbor side of the Banyan Tree Square stands the Old Courthouse, originally built in 1857, and which once served as the center for government activities, including in it, in its basement, a jail. The Courthouse and jail now house — yes — two art galleries. Also of interest at the Banyan Tree Square, directly across from the waterfront, are the remnants of Lahaina's Old Fort, constructed from coral blocks, in 1832. The fort was originally built to deter the rebellious whalers from the whaling ships anchored in the harbor, who were revolting against the town's newly-imposed disciplinary laws. Typically, cannons were mounted on the fort wall, and each night, it is said, a King's soldier would beat a drum atop the fort, as a signal for all seamen to return to their ships or be confined to prison for the night. The fort, however, was used primarily as a prison, until 1854, at which time it was largely dismantled and the coral blocks taken to build the new town jail, Hale Pa'ahao.

Another place of supreme visitor interest, located on Front Street,

MAUI

TO MOLOKAI

Pailolo   *Channel*

Kanounou Pt.   *Nakalele Pt.*

PACIF.

Honolua Bay   30

KAPALUA   HONOKAHUA   *Kahakuloa Bay*
Napili Bay

340

KAHAKULOA

KAHANA

Kahekili

HONOKOWAI   *WEST MAUI AIRPORT*

KAHULUI AIRPORT

340

WAIHEE

KAANAPALI   WAIEHU

PAIA

Kahului Bay

30

WAILUKU   KAHULUI

LAHAINA   *Puu Kukui*   IAO   VALLEY

37   *Haleakala*

30

PUUNENE

Honoapiilani   *Hwy.*

Au'au

PUKALA

Channel

TO LANAI

OLOWALU   *Hwy.*

MAALAEA

30   *Maalaea Bay*

Papawai Pt.

31   *Piilani Hwy.*

KIHEI

KU

Kula Hwy.

WAILEA

ULUPALA RANCH

MOLOKINI

MAKENA

Ahihi-Kinau Natural Area Reserve

Ahihi Bay

KANAIO

La Perouse Bay

Alalakeiki

Channel

TO KAHOOLAWE

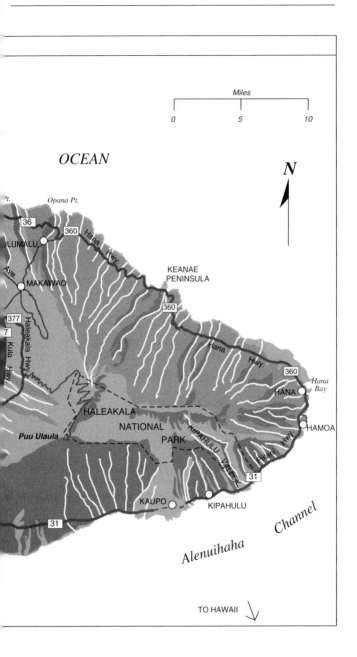

adjacent to the Banyan Tree, is the historic Pioneer Inn, originally built in 1901, some 25 years after the end of the whaling era, but which, nevertheless, is reflective, in its architecture and theme, of Lahaina's whaling period, with vintage whaling equipment and photographs of 19th-century whaling expeditions adorning its walls. The inn, however, it is believed, was originally built at Keomuku, on the nearby island of Lanai, and later on barged across the channel to Lahaina. In any event, the 48-room inn, now largely restored, houses shops and a restaurant and saloon, and has overnight guest accommodations.

Directly across from the Pioneer Inn, docked in the harbor, and also well worth investigating, is the Brig *Carthaginian*, which is in fact a replica — built in the 1920s — of the 19th-century square-riggers that brought the first missionaries from Boston, around the Horn, to Hawaii. The brig now houses a museum, with an exhibit on whales and whaling, and where you can also see films on whaling.

Close at hand, too, on the north side of Pioneer Inn is the site of the Brick Palace, quite possibly the first Western structure on Maui, built by King Kamehameha I, around 1800. Kamehameha was rather intrigued by Western architecture, as, too, he was with Western ships and weapons; but his favorite wife, Queen Ka'ahumanu, refused to live in the enclosed environment of the stone and brick structure, preferring, instead, a native Hawaiian grass hut located adjacent to the "palace." In any case, directly in front of the site of the Brick Palace, in the water, and also with some interest, is the Hauola Stone, bestowed, we are told, with magical healing powers.

For history buffs, there is yet another place of supreme interest. At the corner of Front and Dickenson streets, across from the Pioneer Inn, stands the beautifully restored Baldwin House, built in the 1830s by missionary-physician Reverend Dwight Baldwin, who arrived in Lahaina in 1835, and lived and raised his family here, until his death in 1868. Reverend Baldwin conducted missionary activities as well as his medical practice from this house. The Baldwin House, constructed from coral and rock and plastered over, is now a living museum, filled with original furnishings and several personal and household items of the Baldwin family. The museum is operated by the Lahaina Restoration Foundation, originally established in the 1950s, and which has, over the years, rescued, restored and preserved many of Lahaina's historic buildings.

Adjacent to the Baldwin House, and also of interest, is the Master's Reading Room, where the Lahaina Restoration Foundation now houses its offices. The Master's Reading Room, dating from 1833 and quite possibly Maui's oldest building, was originally used as storage space by missionaries, until, in 1834, the upper story was converted into an officers' club for masters and officers, providing in it, too — as an added bonus — an excellent vantage point from where ships' captains could watch over their fleets and crews. The Reading Room, however, was sold at an auction, in 1846, to Reverend Baldwin, whose growing family then occupied it.

Try to also visit the new prison, Hale Pa'ahao — meaning "stuck-in-irons house" — located on Prison Street, at the corner of

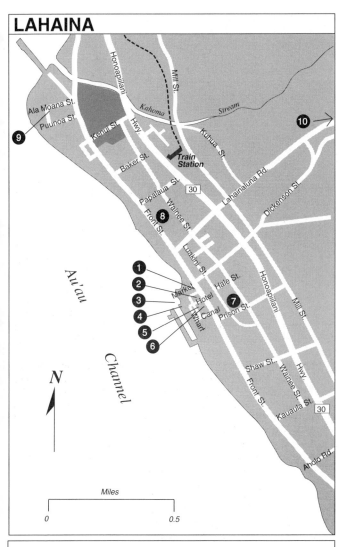

LAHAINA

1. Baldwin House
2. Pioneer Inn
3. Brig Carthaginian II
4. Site of Brick Palace
5. Old Fort and Courthouse
6. Banyan Tree
7. Hale Paahao Prison
8. Wo Hing Society Temple
9. Jodo Mission
10. Lahainaluna Seminary

Waine'e Street. Hale Pa'ahao was originally built in 1854, from coral blocks taken from the Old Fort, and has been largely preserved in its original state, much as it appeared in the 1850s, with one cell displaying a mannequin of an old salt, and another, a list of the convictions handed down over the years, posted on the wall, as well as the diary of an inmate confined to the cell.

South from Hale Pa'ahao on Waine'e Street, and also worth visiting, is the Wailoa Congregational Church, formerly the Waine'e Church, with its associations to Keopuolani, wife to Kamehameha I and mother of Kamehameha II and Kamehameha III, who was one of the first Hawaiians to convert to Christianity at this church. The church, it is interesting to note, was originally built in 1823 and subsequently destroyed and rebuilt several times over the years, the last in 1988, when it was renamed, Wailoa, meaning "living waters." There is a cemetery, the Wailoa Cemetery, located adjacent to the church, where several members of Hawaii's royal family lie buried, as well as some early missionaries and their children.

A little way from the Wailoa Church, at the corner of Front and Shaw streets, is the Malu'uluolele Park, a community park, with a baseball facility and basketball and tennis courts. Interestingly, the park is also the site of the ancient Mokuhinia Pond, which featured a small islet at the center of it, where the royal residences of Kamehameha II and, later on, Kamehameha III once stood. The pond also, we are told, was once the home of Hawaii's legendary *mo'o* (lizard), Kilawahine, which visited all the Hawaiian islands, unifying the bloodlines of all the islands' inhabitants.

Another place of interest, northward from the center of town, on Front Street, is the Wo Hing Society Temple, dating from 1812, and originally built as a fraternal and social meeting hall for Hawaii's Chinese population. The temple now houses a museum devoted to Chinese culture, exhibiting Chinese artifacts, including a Taoist shrine, located on its upper floor. There is also a small, historic theater located adjacent to the temple, the Cookhouse Theatre, which features some fascinating old films of Hawaii, shot by Thomas Edison in 1898.

Just to the north of the center of town, too, about a mile or so, on Ala Moana Street, stands the Jodo Mission, which has in it one of the largest statues of Buddha outside Asia. The statue was erected in 1968, to commemorate the centennial of the arrival of the first Japanese immigrants in Hawaii, in 1868.

Yet another place of interest, eastward from the center of town of Lahaina, some 2 miles on the Lahainaluna Road, which goes off the Honoapi'ilani Highway, is the historic Lahainaluna Seminary, founded in 1831 by missionaries, and with the distinction of being the oldest educational institution in the West. The seminary also has in it one of the oldest printing presses west of the Rockies, the Hale Pai — literally translated, the "House of Printing" — on which, in 1834, the first Hawaiian-language newspaper was printed, as well as texts used at the seminary. Hale Pai now has on display a replica of the original press, as well as the original oak plates and samples of the early type, including some first editions of books printed here in the 1830s.

Interestingly, one of Lahainaluna's most notable graduates was David Malo, acknowledged as Hawaii's first scholar, who also wrote the definitive Hawaiian history, *Hawaiian Antiquities*. Malo foresaw and feared the changing of the Hawaiian culture, and asked to be buried "high above the tide of foreign invasion." His grave can now be seen on the hillside, by the giant "L," above Lahainaluna.

Ka'anapali

From Lahaina, it is 4 miles, directly north on the coastal Honoapi'ilani Highway (30), to Ka'anapali, passing by, approximately midway between Lahaina and Ka'anapali, two roadside beach parks — Wahikuli State Wayside Beach Park and Hanakao'o Beach Park — both with good swimming and snorkeling possibilities, and the latter especially popular with beach-goers.

Alternatively, you can journey to Ka'anapali on board the Lahaina-Ka'anapali & Pacific Railroad — popularly known as the Sugarcane Train — a 19th-century steam train, which once transported sugar from a Lahaina mill to a warehouse just to the north of Black Rock, in Ka'anapali, from where it was then shipped out by boat. The Sugarcane Train, of course, now whisks tourists through cane fields, through an area, between Lahaina and Ka'anapali, that was once devoted wholly to the cultivation of sugarcane. The Sugarcane Train Station in Lahaina, by the way, is located just north of the Lahainaluna Road — which goes off the Honoapi'ilani Highway — on Hinau Road.

In any event, Ka'anapali, it must be fair to say, is one of Hawaii's most popular beach resorts — second only to Oahu's Waikiki — and also the westernmost point on Maui. The Ka'anapali Beach itself is a glorious, 3-mile-long white-sand beach, bordered by world-class, luxury highrise hotels and condominium complexes, developed largely between 1962 and 1987. There are, in fact, six full-fledged hotels here — Hyatt Regency, Westin, Sheraton, Marriott, Ka'anapali Beach Hotel and Royal Lahaina — five condominium complexes, two championship, 18-hole golf courses, dozens of tennis courts, a first-class shopping mall, and several excellent restaurants

Prominent among Ka'anapali's properties, of course, is the splendid, 815-room Hyatt Regency Maui, sprawled over 18½ acres, at the southern end of the Ka'anapali Beach Resort, and developed, in 1980, by Hawaii's famous developer, Chris Hemmeter, at a cost of around $80 million. The hotel boasts five restaurants and six bars, a dazzling lobby with a century-old banyan tree, acres of well-kept gardens — filled with tropical plants, trees and flowers, and exotic birds such as peacocks, penguins, flamingos and swans — lagoons, a half-acre swimming pool with a 2½-story-high waterslide, and some 60 waterfalls, large and small. The hotel also has on display a superb, $2 million art collection, featuring Hawaiian and South Pacific art and rare antiques.

KA'ANAPALI

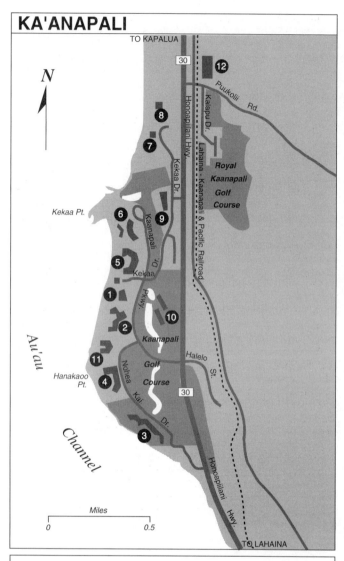

1. Whaler's Village
2. Westin Maui
3. Hyatt Regency
4. Maui Marriott
5. Kaanapali Beach Hotel
6. Sheraton Maui
7. Royal Lahaina
8. Maui Kaanapali Villas
9. Maui Eldorado Resort
10. Kaanapali Royal Hotel
11. Kaanapali Alii
12. Train Station

Just to the north of the Hyatt Regency, on a 15-acre site, sits the Maui Marriott, a 720-room, 9-story hotel, with an open-air lobby that rises four full stories, developed in 1981; and north of there, situated on the beach, is the Westin Maui, the other gem of Ka'anapali, with its two 11-story towers and 761 oceanview rooms, also developed by Chris Hemmeter. The Westin, in fact, was formerly the Maui Surf Hotel, redeveloped in 1987, at a cost of $155 million. It now features 9 restaurants and lounges, landscaped grounds with exotic birds, 5 multi-level swimming pools, waterslides, more than a dozen waterfalls, and an extensive $2.5 million collection of Asian and Pacific art.

Among Ka'anapali's other hotels, lying farther to the north along the Ka'anapali Beach, are the lowrise, 429-room Ka'anapali Beach Hotel; the 503-room Sheraton-Maui, situated on a 23-acre site, and originally developed in 1963; and the 12-story, 545-room Royal Lahaina, the oldest of Ka'anapali's hotels, built in December, 1962.

Besides the resorts, there is more to interest the visitor at Ka'anapali. More or less at the center of the Ka'anapali strip, for instance, lies the Whaler's Village, an outdoor shopping mall with more than 50 shops and restaurants, and — equally important at Ka'anapali — ample parking. A place of special interest at the Whaler's Village, however, is the Whaling Museum, which has some excellent exhibits depicting life during the whaling era, including old photographs, whaling artifacts, and films on the history of Maui's whaling industry.

Another place of interest, at the north end of Ka'anapali Beach, near the Sheraton-Maui, is Black Rock, known to the Hawaiians as a Leina a Kauhane, meaning "soul's leap." Black Rock, in many ways, is a sacred place, where, according to Hawaiian legend, the dying would enter the world of spirits by leaping off the cliffs into the ocean below. The Black Rock area, we might add, also offers some of the best swimming and snorkeling at Maui, especially in calm weather.

Ka'anapali's white-sand beach, of course, continues beyond Black Rock, northward, offering good swimming possibilities, and, yes, fewer people. To access this northern portion of the beach, you can either walk around Black Rock, or go north from Ka'anapali on the Honoapi'ilani Highway, about a mile, then take Puukolii Road off the highway, toward the ocean, and follow the signs to the beach.

North to Kapalua

North from Ka'anapali, the highrise resort development quickly gives way to smaller beach communities — Honokowai and Kahana — cluttered with lowrise condominium complexes, mostly two and three stories, and situated on the Lower Honoapi'ilani Road, which runs parallel to the Honoapi'ilani Highway, to the west, closer to the coast. The beaches along here, too, we might add, are smaller, less attractive, than, say, Ka'anapali Beach to the south, or those farther to the north, at Napili and Kapalua; however, the Honokowai-Kahana coast, it must be fair to say, does offer good, unobstructed views of the nearby islands of Lanai and Molokai. Besides which, as an added bonus to the budget-minded traveler, the area, quite typically, offers more affordable accommodations than the Ka'anapali and Kapalua resorts.

Farther still, north of Honokowai and Kahana, a mile or two, lies Napili Bay, which has a delightful, palm-fringed white-sand beach, with excellent swimming and snorkeling possibilities, and superb views, across the Pailolo Channel, of Molokai. Napili Bay also offers good golf — at nearby Kapalua — and tennis facilities, as well as some shopping possibilities and one or two worthwhile restaurants.

Adjoining to the north of Napili Bay, of course, is Kapalua, one of West Maui's most prestigious resorts, originally developed in the mid-1970s by the Maui Land & Pineapple Company, and built around the lovely, crescent-shaped white-sand Kapalua Beach — which, again, offers excellent swimming and snorkeling possibilities. The centerpiece of the resort, however, is the exclusive — and, yes, expensive — 194-room Kapalua Bay Hotel, which, needless to say, has commanding views of the ocean on nearly all sides, backing on to a wooded, 18-hole golf course and, happily, fields of pineapple. There are also tennis courts here, and first-class shops and restaurants. In addition to which, the Kapalua Resort includes in it two luxury condominium complexes, the 118-unit Kapalua Villas and the 40-unit Ironwoods.

Northeastward from Kapalua on the Honoapi'ilani Highway, a mile or so — past mile marker 31 — is Honokahua Bay, at the head of which lies the D.T. Fleming Beach Park, a popular beach, named for David T. Fleming, a manager at the nearby Honolua Ranch in the early 1900s, and who, most notably, helped introduce pineapple as a commercial crop in West Maui. The beach has picnic tables and showers and restrooms, and, occasionally, it also offers some surfing possibilities; swimming, however, is not encouraged, due to the strong undercurrents which make the sport rather unsafe. Near the beach, too, behind the sand dunes just to the south, is an ancient Hawaiian burial site, where skeletal remains were unearthed when construction began on a new hotel. The hotel — the Ritz Carlton — subsequently relocated to a site farther inland, and the burial site is now being restored.

West Maui's North Coast

The coastal stretch north from Honokahua Bay to Honokohau Bay, and, again, from Honokohau Bay southeastward toward Wailuku, is rather lovely, largely unspoiled and remarkably picturesque, with rugged cliffs overhanging the ocean and lush valleys and pasturelands fanning out inland, and breathtaking views to be encountered at every turn of the highway (which, here, is still the Honoapi'ilani Highway). Indeed, the coastal stretch along here offers the motorist-adventurer a rare opportunity to experience pristine Hawaii.

WEST MAUI'S NORTH COAST

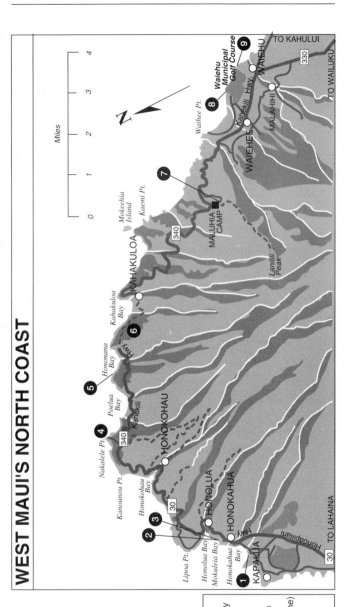

1. D.T. Fleming Beach
2. Honolua-Mokuleia Bay
   Marine Life
   Conservation District
3. Mokuleia Beach
4. Nakalele Light Station
5. Blowhole
6. Pohaku Kani (Bellstone)
7. Waihee Trailhead
8. Waihee Beach
9. Waiehu Beach

In any case, first off, a little over a mile from Honokahua Bay —
just past mile marker 32 — and reached by way of a small trail
leading from the highway turnout down to the ocean, is Mokuleia
Beach, popularly known as Slaughterhouse Beach, for its treacherous waves which, especially in the winter months, can be seen
pounding, vengefully, the small, sandy beach below. Mokuleia,
nevertheless, locals will tell you, is *the* place for bodysurfing during
the summer months.

Mokuleia Beach, of course, lies at the head of Mokuleia Bay,
adjoining to the north of which is Honolua Bay, which, together,
form the Honolua-Mokuleia Bay Marine Life Conservation District,
where removal or molestation of any marine life, shell rocks or
corals is prohibited, making this an excellent area for snorkeling,
especially in calm seas. Interestingly, it is also possible to snorkel or
swim from one bay to the other, around Kalaepiha Point, which
separates the two bays.

Honolua Bay, we might add, is also one of Hawaii's foremost
surfing spots, second only to Oahu's North Shore, and which has,
over the years, been featured on several surfing posters and covers
of surfing magazines. For spectators, of course, there is Lipoa Point
— reached by way of a dirt trail that dashes off the highway, a
half-mile or so past mile marker 33, and journeys along the east side
of the bay to the top of the headland — which has a bird's-eye view
of the bay below, and from where you can watch world-class surfers
challenge some of the most spectacular waves, especially in the
winter months.

Three miles from Honolua Bay on the Honoapi'ilani Highway,
northeastward, and we are at Honokohau Bay, which has very little
of interest, save for a small, rocky beach that attracts a handful of
surfers. Honokohau Bay, however, is important in that it marks the
end of the Honoapi'ilani Highway (30) and the beginning of the
Kahekili Highway (340), which journeys along the backside of West
Maui, skirting the West Maui Mountains on the northeast, some 22
miles southeastward to Wailuku, taking in, too, at least 2 miles of
unpaved road that can often be impassable, especially during rainy
weather.

Eastward from Honokohau on the Kahekili Highway, however, 2
miles or so, a small side road — accessed only on foot — dashes off
toward the ocean, to the Nakalele Light Station, situated on a grassy
slope — ideally suited to picnicking and strolling around — that
tumbles down to the cliffs, at the bottom of which you can see a
series of rock arches and natural pools. Also of interest, some $2\frac{1}{2}$
miles from the light station, just off the highway, on the ocean side,
is a lookout, which has good views of a blowhole.

South from the blowhole, another $1\frac{1}{2}$ miles, the paved road
finally ends, and a little way from there, a half mile or so, just off
the highway, with a rusty old sign pointing to it, is Pohaku Kani —
the Bellstone — a six-foot-high boulder, which, we are told, if struck
in a certain manner, can resound throughout the adjacent valley.

Farther still, a little over a mile, at Kahakuloa — a tiny fishing
village with a handful of houses, taro patches, and two or three

churches — the paved road begins again. From Kahakuloa, it is another 7 miles, approximately, to the "Maluhia Camp" turnoff, from where a narrow, mile-long side road leads through rolling pastures to the Waihe'e Trailhead, at the head of the 3-mile Waihe'e Ridge Trail that leads to the Lanilili peak, elevation 2,563 feet. The trail is somewhat strenuous, climbing roughly 1,500 feet over the 3 miles, but well worth the effort, with good, all-round views to be enjoyed from the top.

Southeastward from the Waihe'e Trail turnoff, some 2 miles, on the *makai* side of the highway, is Waihe'e Point, which has superb views of the coastline below, and south of there are the sleepy little towns of Waihe'e, about a mile from Waihe'e Point, and Waiehu, another 2 miles or so from Waihe'e. Waihe'e and Waiehu each have a beach park, frequented primarily by fishermen, and a golf course, besides, situated more or less midway between the two towns.

From Waiehu, Kahekili Highway heads directly south to Wailuku, passing by, just to the north of Wailuku, the Halekii-Pihana Heiaus State Monument — reached by way of Waiehu Beach Road, which goes off the highway, then Kuhio Place southwestward, off Waiehu Beach Road, and Hea Place south off Kuhio Place to Halekii Heiau, the first of the *heiaus*, situated on small hill by the Iao Stream; Pihana Heiau is just to the south of the Halekii Heiau, at the end of a short trail. The *heiaus*, of course, are significant, historically, in that Maui's King Kahekili once lived here, and, also, Queen Kepuolani, wife of Kamehameha I and mother of Kamehameha II, was born here. From the Halekii-Pihana *heiaus*, you can return to Waiehu Beach Road or the Kahekili Highway, both important arteries, and so to Wailuku.

Lahaina to Ma'alaea

It is approximately 15 miles from Lahaina south to Ma'alaea, journeying along West Maui's south coast, on the Honoapi'ilani Highway (30), with the West Maui Mountains on one side, and the ocean on the other. The coastal stretch, quite typically, is dotted with a handful of small beach parks — many of which offer swimming, snorkeling and picnicking possibilities — and one or two lookouts, adding to the interest of the motorist. From Ma'alaea, it is another 6 miles or so northward, across the isthmus, to Wailuku, in East Maui.

In any case, northernmost on the route, a mile or so south from Lahaina, is the Puamana Beach Park, a grassy park with a narrow strip of sand, which offers good swimming and, occasionally, surfing possibilities; and a mile south of there lies Launiupoko State Wayside Park, which has a small sandy beach, a man-made children's wading pool, picnic tables, barbecue grills, and showers and restrooms. The Launiupoko park also has excellent views of the islands of Lanai and Kaho'olawe, just to the west and south, respectively.

Some 3 miles farther, southeastward, lies Olowalu, a village, no more, notable as the site of the 1790 Olowalu Massacre, which resulted when a longboat was stolen from an American ship by

Hawaiians, primarily for its iron content, and, in retaliation, the American captain, Simon Metcalf, deceptively lured the Hawaiians into approaching his ship, and opened fire on them, killing more than a hundred Hawaiians. Olowalu, however, now has in it a general store and a French restaurant, Chez Paul. Besides which, a small cane road leads from here — from near the water tank located behind the general store — a half-mile *mauka* — toward the mountains — to some petroglyphs, depicting human figures and various animals.

South from Olowalu, another mile or so, lies Punahoa Beach, an essentially undeveloped roadside beach, bordered by native *kiawe* trees. Punahoa has some good snorkeling — and, at times, also surfing — possibilities.

Just to the south of the Punahoa Beach, 2 miles, is the Ukume-hame Beach Park, with its narrow, rocky coastal strip, frequented primarily by fishermen; and another half-mile south of there, situated just off the highway, is the Papalaua State Wayside Park, also undeveloped, and backing onto groves of *kiawe*. The Papalaua beach park, by the way, offers picnicking and surfing possibilities.

Farther still, another 3 miles southeastward, and we are at Papawai Point, the southernmost point on West Maui, where there is a lookout, with good views of Molokini and Kaho'olawe to the south, and Haleakala farther to the southeast. Papawai Point, we might add, is also an excellent place for whale watching, in season (November-May), from where you can see the humpback whales and their calves frolicking in the ocean, just off shore.

Finally, some 3 or 4 miles farther, as the highway turns northeastward, there is Ma'alaea, a small boat harbor, from where you can take boat excursions or fishing trips out to sea. From Ma'alaea, too, you can continue northward on the Honoapi'ilani Highway to Wailuku, or return to Lahaina, on the same route.

SOUTHWEST COAST

Kihei

Northernmost on East Maui's southwest coast, some 19 miles southwestward from Lahaina (or 7 miles south of Kahului), is Kihei, historically important as a landing for Hawaiian war canoes, and with its associations to British explorer, Captain George Vancouver, who first landed here in 1792, and returned the following year, in 1793, bringing with him live cattle and root vegetables, which he introduced to Maui. There is a monument commemorating Vancouver's first landing here, located on the ocean side of South Kihei Road, directly across from Maui Lui Hotel.

Kihei, it must be fair to say, has no real town center as such; South Kihei Road runs directly north-south through the town, beginning at the intersection of Mokulele Highway (350) and Pi'ilani Highway (31), and continuing south toward Wailea. On one side of it — the

The Iao Needle, in the Iao Valley State Park, rises 1,200 feet vertically from the valley floor

Windsurfing at Hookipa Beach Park, just east of Paia

ocean side — stand the hotels and a haphazard jumble of condominiums, and on the *mauka* — inland — side, shopping centers. This is not to say, however, that Kihei is without visitor interest; on the contrary, it has some six miles of sandy beaches, with views of West Maui and the nearby islands of Lanai, Kaho'olawe and Molokini — a partially-submerged crescent-shaped crater, rising 150 feet from the ocean, and now a protected marine reserve and seabird sanctuary, quite popular with scuba divers and snorkeling enthusiasts, located just offshore, to the southwest.

Prominent among Kihei's beaches, situated just to the north of Kihei, off North Kihei Road (Highway 31), is Ma'alaea Beach, all of 3 miles long, with several access points, ideal for beachcombing and jogging, especially in the mornings; and across from there, on the *mauka* side of the highway, is the Kealia Pond Bird Sanctuary, a 300-acre wildlife refuge, where you can see, among others species of birds, Hawaiian stilts and coots, both indigenous waterfowl.

Among other beaches in Kihei are Maipoina Oe lau, a narrow roadside beach, and a good place for whale watching during the winter months, situated just off South Kihei Road, a half mile south of the intersection of Mokulele Highway; and Kalepolepo Beach, another half mile south on the South Kihei Road, with some swimming possibilities. This last, the Kalepolepo Beach, by the way, is also the site of the ancient Ko'ie'ie Fishpond, where you can still see the fishpond walls intact.

Another place of interest here, quite close to the Maipoina Oe lau and Kalepolepo beaches and also the Vancouver Monument, located a half mile or so on the Kulanihakoi Road, is the Trinity Church by the Sea, originally the site of Hawaiian scholar David Malo's Kilolani Church, where Malo once preached outdoors. The church, of course, was reorganized in 1976, and, in keeping with tradition, services are still held there, outdoors.

South still, 4 or 5 miles, are the Kama'ole I, Kama'ole II and Kama'ole III beaches, with restrooms, showers and picnic tables, and good swimming possibilities — except during heavy surf or kona storms. Kama'ole I Beach, the northernmost of the three, also offers excellent bodysurfing possibilities, near its north end — a section of the beach known as Young's Beach; while the Kama'ole III Beach features a playground area, especially interesting to children.

Wailea

South from Kihei, approximately 2 miles, lies Wailea, a well-planned, exclusive resort, fronting on a lovely, 2-mile-long white-sand beach, and reached on either the well-traveled South Kihei Road — which eventually becomes Wailea Alanui — or by way of the by-pass route, Pi'ilani Highway (31). In any event, Wailea has six world-class, luxury hotels — the Inter-Continental, Stouffer's, Four Seasons, the Grand Hyatt, Embassy Suites and Kea Lani — several plush condominiums, and an excellent shopping center, the Wailea Shopping Village. It also has three championship, 18-hole

KIHEI - MAKENA

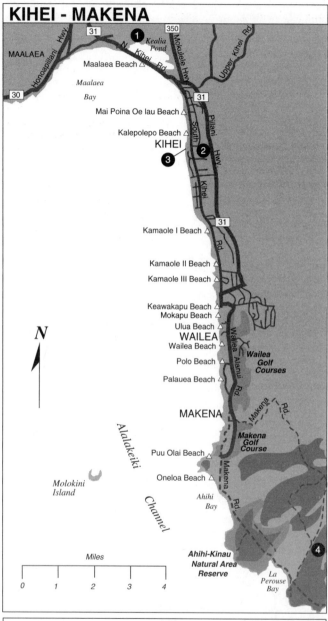

1. Kealia Pond Bird Sanctuary
2. David Malo's Kiolani Church
3. Koieie Fishpond
4. Site of 1790 Lava Flow

golf courses, notable among them the Blue Course, site of the LPGA Women's Kemper Open, held in February; and scores of tennis courts, including those at the Wailea Tennis Club, billed as "Wimbledon West."

Among Wailea's hotels, of course, Stouffer's Wailea Beach Hotel is perhaps most notable, originally built in 1978 as the Westin, and purchased, in 1983, by Stouffer Hotels, and upgraded a few years later, in 1987, at a cost of $7 million. The lowrise 347-room hotel now boasts, besides its oceanview rooms with lanais, beautifully landscaped gardens, waterfalls, pool, whirlpool spas, 3 restaurants, an art-decorated lobby, and golf and tennis facilities. Additionally, the beach at Stouffer's has excellent swimming, snorkeling, windsurfing and sunbathing possibilities.

Wailea's other notable resort hotel is the 600-room Maui Inter-Continental Hotel, the first hotel to be developed at the Wailea Resort, in 1976. The hotel consists of one 7-story and 6 lowrise buildings, three swimming pools, golf and tennis facilities, and four excellent restaurants. The hotel also offers its very own helicopter tours of the island.

Wailea also has some excellent, sandy beaches — Keawakapu, Mokapu, Ulua, Wailea and Polo — which are in fact part of the 2-mile strip bordering the resort development. They are, nevertheless, less crowded than the beaches farther north at Kihei, and offer some of the best swimming, snorkeling and bodysurfing on the island. The beaches are also remarkably easily accessible, with well-marked access roads dashing off Wailea's main street, Wailea Alanui.

Makena

South from Wailea, the Wailea Alanui Road becomes Makena Alanui, and leads directly to Makena, a little over 2 miles distant. Makena, quite typically, is less developed than either Wailea or Kihei, with *kiawe* trees lining its beaches, rather than resort developments, and with wild sort of roads, largely unmarked, leading off to the beaches. Makena does, however, have one or two good hotels and condominiums, notable among them the Maui Prince Hotel, a relatively new, luxury hotel, developed in 1986, offering 300 oceanfront guest rooms — with views of the islands of Lanai, Kaho'olawe and Molokini — three well-appointed restaurants, two swimming pools, and golf and tennis facilities. The hotel also features a delightful Japanese water garden, with fish ponds, smaller rock gardens, waterfalls, and small pagodas.

Makena also has some good sandy beaches, well worth exploring. The Oneloa Beach, for one, commonly known as Makena Beach — and also "Big Beach" — is perhaps one of the area's loveliest — an idyllic, white-sand beach, a half mile long, reached by way of Makena Alanui, some 3 miles south from the intersection of Kaukahi Road in Wailea, then off on a dirt road, heading *makai*, another quarter mile or so to the beach. Interestingly, in the early 1970s, nearly a hundred people — hippies in search of an alternative lifestyle — inhabited the beach.

Adjoining to the north of Makena Beach, and separated by the 360-foot-high cinder cone, Pu'u Olai, is Pu'u Olai Beach, also known as Little Beach. A trail leads over the rocky outcropping, from Makena — or Big — Beach to Little Beach, the latter a lovely, crescent-shaped beach, with excellent swimming and bodysurfing possibilities, as well as some promising snorkeling, on calm days, around Pu'u Olai Point. Little Beach, by the way, is also quite popular with nudists, although — a word of caution — Hawaii's state laws prohibit nude bathing at public beaches.

South still, another mile or two on Makena Road — which is really a continuation of Makena Alanui — lies the Ahihi-kina'u Natural Area Reserve, a 2,045-acre preserve, which includes in it an 807-acre undersea ecological reserve, originally established in 1979. Ahihi-Kinau, interestingly, is also the site of the last lava flow on the island, which occurred in 1790, making this a rather barren tract of land, covered with a hard lava crust. The park, however, is a good place for snorkeling and scuba diving, especially when the ocean is calm.

Also of interest, one and one-half miles south of Ahihi-kina'u, at the end of Makena Road, is La Perouse Bay, named for French nobleman and navigator, Compte de la Perouse, the first European to land on Maui, in 1786. La Perouse Bay, however, is a beautiful but desolate place, popular, primarily, with fishermen and divers. From La Perouse Bay, too, the historic Hoapili Trail — or "King's Highway" — heads out east, passing by, near the bay itself, the ruins of an ancient fishing village. The trail, in fact, begins roughly three-quarters of a mile from the end of the paved Makena Road — with a large white sign, standing in the midst of the hardened lava, indicating the trailhead — and journeys some 2 miles through the lava flow area, to the secluded, rocky Kanaio Beach, more or less at the southern tip of the island.

CENTRAL MAUI

Kahului and Wailuku

Kahului, together with the adjoining city of Wailuku, is the commercial center of Maui, with most of the island's shops, shopping centers, restaurants and other facilities located there, mostly concentrated on Ka'ahumanu Avenue, the city's main street, which runs directly east-west, and northeast-southwest, through the heart of the city. Kahului, we might add, is also Maui's only deep-water port, from where all the island's sugar and pineapple are shipped, and where most of the freighters and cruise ships bound for Maui arrive, docking in the Kahului Harbor. Besides which, Maui's main airport, the Kahului Airport, is situated just to the east of the city, at the end of Keolani Place, some 2 or 3 miles distant.

For visitors, Kahului has one or two places of interest, notably the Kanaha Pond State Wildlife Sanctuary, located on the Hana Highway (36), near the intersection of the Haleakala Highway (396), just to the east of the city center, and where you can see indigenous Hawaiian stilts and Hawaiian coots, and other endangered species; and the Kanaha Beach County Park, located just off Alahao Street, which goes off Ka'a Street, which, in turn, goes off Keolani Place (Highway 380), northeastward. This last, the Kanaha Beach County Park, bordered by ironwoods and protected by a coral reef, has good picnicking and swimming possibilities, especially for children, and is also quite popular with windsurfing enthusiasts, of all ages and abilities.

South from Kahului, too, on Pu'unene Avenue (Highway 350), a mile or so, lies Pu'unene, a satellite community of Kahului, which has in it, located at the corner of Pu'unene Avenue and Hansen Road, and of interest to the visitor, the Alexander & Baldwin Sugar Museum, where you can see several sugar industry-related artifacts as well as scale models of the sugar factory, and also learn about sugar production — from the planting and harvesting of the sugarcane, to the processing and bagging of the sugar. The museum also has on display portraits of members of the Alexander and Baldwin families, together with the family histories, as well as old photographs of men, women and children who worked in the company's sugarcane fields and factory. The museum, interestingly, is housed in the former home of the factory superintendent, surrounded by sugarcane fields, and directly across the street from there stands the Hawaiian Commercial & Sugar Mill, formerly the Alexander & Baldwin sugar mill, still in operation.

Adjoining to the west of Kahului, of course, is Wailuku, the seat of Maui County (which includes not only the island of Maui, but also Molokai, Lanai and Kaho'olawe). Wailuku is also an historic town, with several old, historic buildings still there, mostly concentrated in its designated Historical District, on High, Market and Vineyard streets. Here, for instance, at the corner of High and Main streets, directly across from the Wailuku Courthouse, you can search out the New England-style Ka'ahumanu Church, built in 1837 and named for Queen Ka'ahumanu, one of the wives of King Kamehameha I, and an important convert to Christianity, who helped bring the religion into acceptance on Maui. The church, by the way, has Hawaiian services — yes, in Hawaiian! — on Sundays.

Close at hand, too, just west of the Ka'ahumanu Church, and also on Main Street, is Hale Hoikeike — the "House of Display" — built between 1833 and 1850, and which was formerly the house of New England missionary Edward Bailey, who arrived in Maui in 1840, together with his wife, to teach at the Wailuku Female Seminary which was established here in 1833. Hale Hoikeike is now a museum, and home to the Maui Historical Society. It houses in it displays centered around Hawaiian and missionary history, as well as a collection of Reverend Bailey's art, depicting scenes from the 1800s.

KAHULUI - WAILUKU

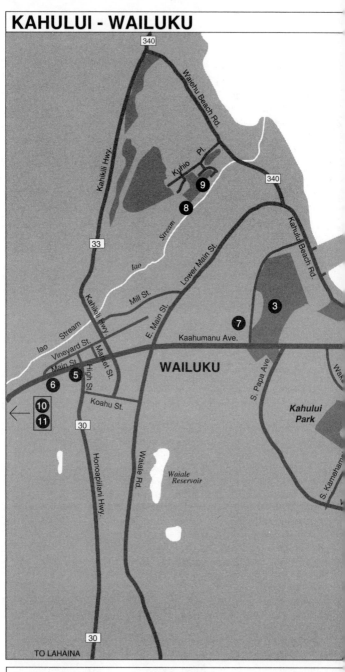

1. Kanaha Pond State Wildlife Sanctuary
2. Kanaha Beach Park
3. Maui Zoological & Botanical Gardens
4. Alexander & Baldwin Sugar Museum
5. Kaahumanu Church
6. Hale Hoikeike (Bailey Museum)

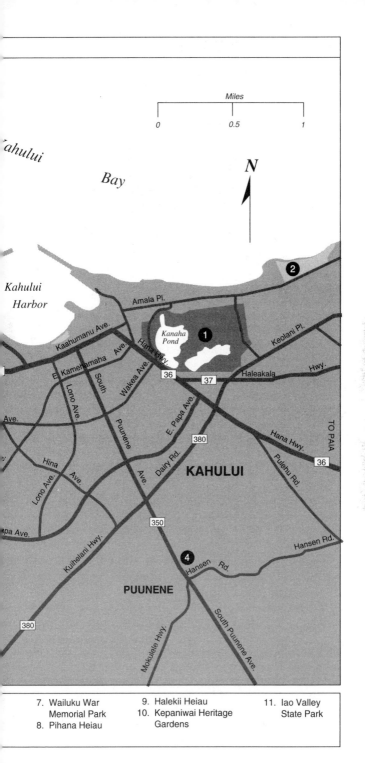

Kahului Bay

Kahului Harbor

Amala Pl.

Kanaha Pond

Kaahumanu Ave.

E. Kamehameha Ave.

South Ave.

Wakea Ave.

Hana Hwy.

Keolani Pl.

36

37

Haleakala Hwy.

Lono Ave.

Puunene Ave.

E. Papa Ave.

380

Dairy Rd.

KAHULUI

Hana Hwy.

Pulehu Rd.

36

TO PAIA

Hina Ave.

Lono Ave.

Ave.

...pa Ave.

Kuihelani Hwy.

350

Hansen Rd.

4

Hansen Rd.

PUUNENE

380

Mokulele Hwy.

South Puunene Ave.

Miles
0   0.5   1

N

| 7. Wailuku War Memorial Park | 9. Halekii Heiau | 11. Iao Valley State Park |
| 8. Pihana Heiau | 10. Kepaniwai Heritage Gardens | |

Also of interest, located on Market Street, near the corner of Main Street, is the Iao Theater, built in 1927, and used, variously, over the years, as a movie theater and playhouse. There are, besides, other buildings of historic note here as well, scattered throughout the historical district, and which can be toured quite at random.

Also in Wailuku, a quarter mile north on Kanaloa Avenue — which goes off Ka'ahumanu Avenue — directly across from the Wailuku War Memorial Park, are the Maui Zoological and Botanical Gardens, especially interesting to children. The zoo, quite typically, has some exotic birds, including peacocks, and monkeys, goats and other such animals; and the botanical gardens feature a small display of indigenous Hawaiian flowers and plants.

In any case, westward from Wailuku lies the lush Iao Valley, reached more or less directly on Main Street and the Iao Valley Road, along a rather scenic drive, with mountains rising on either side of the road. But before reaching the valley, a half-mile or so from the Wailuku township, and of interest, too, are the Tropical Gardens of Maui, where you can see several plants and trees indigenous to the Hawaiian islands. There is also a snack bar and gift shop at the gardens.

From the Tropical Gardens, it is another mile, approximately, to the Kepaniwai Park, located in the valley, and which has in it sections of art and architecture, depicting the ethnic and cultural diversity of the island. Here, for instance, you can see a typical Hawaiian grass hut, a Japanese pagoda surrounded by Japanese gardens and sculpture, a Portuguese villa, a New England salt-box, and Chinese, Filipino and Korean dwellings. The park also offers good picnicking and walking possibilities.

Ironically, however, Kepaniwai has a tragic past. It was the scene of a bloody massacre in 1790, when King Kamehameha I invaded Maui, in his bid to subjugate and unite all the Hawaiian islands under his reign. Kamehameha, it is told, landed his war canoes in Kahului, then drove the island's defenders back into Iao Valley, where they were mercilessly slaughtered. There were, in fact, so many islanders killed, that their bodies filled the Iao Stream; hence the name, Kepaniwai, meaning, "damming of the waters."

A half mile or so west of Kepaniwai, on Iao Valley Road, there is a turnout, from where you can see what many will tell you is the naturally-sculpted profile of John F. Kennedy. The profile can be discerned on a black rock farther into the gorge. There is also a viewfinder here, on the side of the road, to help you locate and focus on the profile.

Farther still, another quarter mile from the John F. Kennedy profile, at the end of Iao Valley Road, lies the Iao Valley State Park, a 4-acre park, which has at the center of it, as its chief attraction, the Iao Needle — a moss-covered, stone spire, that rises some 1,200 feet vertically from the valley floor (or 2,250 feet above sea level). There is also a trail that loops through the park, offering visitors abundant opportunities to view the Iao Needle, as well as explore the surrounding area, criss-crossed by streams and dotted with natural pools and guava trees and wild, yellow ginger plants.

The valley, of course, extends farther back toward the West Maui Mountains, to the extinct volcano, Pu'u Kukui, with an elevation of 5,788 feet, which, by the way, is the highest point in West Maui, and which, we might add, also has the distinction of being one of the wettest spots on earth, with an average annual rainfall of over 400 inches!

From Wailuku, too, 3 miles south on the Honoapi'ilani Highway (30), you can visit Maui's Tropical Plantation, situated on a 120-acre estate in the Waikapu Valley. The plantation is of course one of Maui's foremost tourist attractions, and a showcase of Hawaii's bounty of fruits and nuts; and here, a tram whisks visitors through groves of mango, guava, papaya, banana and macadamia nut trees, and sections of coffee and flowers such as orchids and hibiscus, and pineapple and sugarcane fields. There is also a restaurant at the plantation, the Tropical Restaurant, which features all-you-can-eat tropical luncheon buffets; and the Made-on-Maui Marketplace, where you can buy fresh, locally-grown Valley Island produce. The Tropical Plantation is open to the public daily, 8 a.m. to 5 p.m.

UPCOUNTRY

Upcountry comprises, broadly, the western slopes of Mt. Haleakala. It is of course a lovely area, characteristic in its green pasture lands, dotted quite randomly with cattle, and its fertile soil where much of Hawaii's fruit, vegetables and flowers are grown — quite in contrast to Maui's famous white-sand beaches. Upcountry also, we might add, enjoys significantly cooler temperatures — typically 5°-15° — than the coastal areas of the island. Besides which, it also has several vista points with good, unobstructed views of West Maui and the Kihei-Wailea coast.

South to Makawao

There are two routes by which to reach Upcountry from central Maui. The first of these leads directly from Kahului, along the Haleakala Highway (37), some 8 miles south to the town of Pukalani, the first town reached in Upcountry. Pukalani means "hole in the clouds," a name which, locals will tell you, is derived from the fact that the town always seems to have the sun shining on it, with clouds rarely lingering overhead. Pukalani itself, however, has very little to interest the visitor, but is a good base from which to explore the Haleakala National Park.

An alternate route into Upcountry is by way of Paia (just east of Kahului), on Baldwin Avenue (Highway 390), south to Makawao, approximately 7 miles. This latter route, of course, has some added attractions. Just a mile from the center of Paia, for instance, on Baldwin Avenue, is the historic Paia Sugar Mill, the oldest continuously operating sugar mill on Maui, originally built around the turn of the century; and south of there, another mile or so, is the beautiful, red-brick Holy Rosary Church, where there is a statue of Father Damien, noted for his humanitarian work in the once-dreaded leper colony on the nearby island of Molokai. Also of interest, quite close at hand, is the Makawao Union Church, built in 1869, and with a lovely stained-glass window.

Yet another place of interest to the visitor to the area, a mile or so south of the Union Church on the highway, is the Baldwin Memorial Home, formerly the home of plantation owners Henry and Ethel Baldwin, built in 1917. The home has in it the Hui Noeau Visual Arts Center, which features a variety of art shows and workshops, and several classes on ceramics, landscape painting, jewelry making, and the like.

Another one and one-half miles on Highway 390, and we are at Makawao — in Upcountry. Makawao, interestingly, is an old Hawaiian cowboy town, which still boasts a few real *paniolos* — Hawaiian cowboys — who often ride into town on horseback for their supplies. The town also hosts what has become the largest rodeo in the state of Hawaii, held on the Fourth of July each year, at the Oskie Rice Arena, on Olinda Road (Highway 390), roughly a mile south of town. The rodeo features a variety of Western events, as well as a parade through town.

Makawao also, it must be fair to say, is a town that is best explored on foot, filled with shops and restaurants, its wood-frame buildings with false fronts reminiscent of the Old West, and interspersed, quite strangely, with yoga centers and herbalists, offering a unique contrast between two very different worlds.

From Makawao, a worthwhile detour is Olinda, journeying south on the Olinda Road, just past the Oskie Rice Arena, along a 9-mile loop that leads through groves of eucalyptus and pine, to finally emerge on Pi'iholo Road — Highway 394 — at the very bottom, then northward again, back to Makawao.

From Makawao, too, you can follow Highway 365, some 2 miles, directly west to Pukalani, then south on the all-important Haleakala Highway, to Kula, the Haleakala National Park, and Ulupalakua Ranch and the Tedeschi Vineyards.

Kula

Kula — at an elevation of 3,000 feet — lies approximately 6 miles south of Pukalani, reached by way of either the Kula Highway (37) or the Haleakala Highway (377). Kula is an area rich in agriculture, where much of Maui's vegetables are grown, including such staples as Maui red onions, potatoes, lettuce and tomatoes. In fact, a little over century ago, at the start of the historic California Gold Rush, the Kula country even supplied California with a substantial portion of its potato needs, earning for itself the name, "Nu Kalifornia."

Kula is also abundant in flowers. Most of the carnations used in leis throughout Hawaii are grown here. Besides which, the area is

UPCOUNTRY

1. Hookipa Beach Park
2. Paia Sugar Mill
3. Holy Rosary Church
4. Baldwin Memorial Home
5. Maui Enchanting Gardens
6. Cloud's Rest Protea Farm
7. Sunrise Protea Farm
8. Kula Botanical Gardens
9. Polipoli Springs State Recreation Area
10. Tedeschi Vineyards
11. Makee Sugar Mill
12. Site of Maui's last eruption (1790)

43

home to the exotic protea, originally brought to Hawaii from Australia and South Africa. The proteas flourish on Kula's mountain slopes, and are among Hawaii's most beautiful flowers, growing in a variety of shapes, sizes and colors. The proteas also make for excellent gifts.

There are several protea farms in the Kula country, open to public tours, many of them located along the Haleakala Highway, notable among them the Hawaii Protea Cooperative, Sunrise Market & Protea Farm and Cloud's Rest Protea Farm. Also on the Haleakala Highway, near the intersection of the Kula Highway, are the Kula Botanical Gardens, where you can view a variety of plants and flowers — including protea, orchids and several types of ginger — as well as native kukui and koa trees, the latter especially prized for its wood, used in handcrafted Hawaiian furniture and wooden bowls.

Of interest, too, south from Kula, some 5 miles, is the Polipoli Springs State Recreation Area, situated on the southwestern slopes of Haleakala, at an elevation of around 6,200 feet, and reached on the mountainous Waipoli Road — partly unpaved — which goes off southeast from the Haleakala Highway, a half-mile or so above the intersection of the Kula Highway (37) and Haleakala Highway. The park itself is quite lovely, largely forested, with groves of pine, cypress, eucalyptus, and towering redwoods. The park also has several miles of wooded hiking trails, as well as camping facilities.

Also south from Kula on the Kula Highway is Keokea, a small town with one or two stores and a well-liked local eatery; and roughly six miles south of there lies the Ulupalakua Ranch, a 20,000-acre working ranch, with approximately 500 cattle, 1,000 sheep and 40 elk. In the late 1800s, the ranch was owned by pioneer James Makee, who planted much of the acreage to sugarcane; but following Makee's death, the new owners transformed Ulupalakua into the present-day ranch.

At the Ulupalakua Ranch, of interest to the visitor, are the Tedeschi Vineyards, Hawaii's only winery, located more or less at the center of the ranch on the Kula Highway. The winery is owned and operated by former Napa Valley vintners, Emil and Jo Ann Tedeschi, who arrived here in 1973 and began experimenting with grape varieties, and found the Carnelian grape to be best suited to the Upcountry soil and climate. The Tedeschis now offer four different grape wines, including two sparkling wines, and — you guessed it — a pineapple wine. There is also a tasting room at the winery, housed in a century-old jailhouse. Of interest, too, directly across the street from the winery, are the ruins of the old Makee Sugar Mill, originally built in 1878, and well worth investigating.

South from the Ulupalakua Ranch, Kula Highway becomes the Pi'ilani Highway (31), and journeys along a desolate section of the island — skirting the southwest corner of Haleakala — toward Hana, offering, enroute, some spectacular views of Kaho'olawe Island and Molokini, which lie just offshore. The highway also passes over a section of lava flow from Haleakala — the last eruption on Maui — which occurred in 1790. The lava flow, in fact, extends all the way south to La Perouse Bay and the Ahihi-Kina'u Natural Area Reserve.

In any event, some 19 miles from the Tedeschi Winery the paved road ends, and not until another 7 miles or so farther, at Kipahulu, does it resume. The unpaved section of the highway, however, is not entirely impassable — especially in dry weather — and it has on it, at an approximate midway point, some one and one-half miles along, the tiny village of Kaupo, inhabited by only a handful of *paniolos* — Hawaiian cowboys. At Kaupo, too, a dirt road dashes off toward the ocean, to the picturesque Huialoha Church, situated on a wind-swept peninsula, and dating from 1859. Also at Kaupo, you can search out the small, quaint Kaupo Store, decorated with antique cameras and other vintage photographic equipment; and a handful of *heiaus*, the Hale O Kane Heiau, Popoiwi Heiau and Lo'alo'a Heiau, the last of these dating from the 16th century.

Six miles farther, and we are at Kipahulu, where the paved highway begins again, continuing northeastward toward Hana.

Haleakala

No tour of Maui would be complete without a visit to the spectacular Mt. Haleakala — "House of the Sun" — the world's largest dormant volcano, situated in the 27,284-acre Haleakala National Park, in the southeast part of the island, and reached on Highway 377, southeastward from Pukalani, some 6 miles, then Highway 378 — the Haleakala Crater Road — westward, along a steep, winding route, another 12 miles, directly into the park. Alternatively, if you are already at Kula, you can take Highway 377 northeastward, roughly 3 miles, then west on Highway 378, and so to the Haleakala park. From the park entrance, it is another 10 miles or so south on the Haleakala Crater Road, climbing another 3,200 feet, approximately, to the summit, Pu'u Ulaula — "Red Hill" — passing by, along the way, the Leleiwi and Kalahaku overlooks, at elevations of 8,000 feet and 9,000 feet, respectively, the latter with some silverswords — a rare flower stalk, 3-8 feet tall, with pointed, silvery leaves, which blooms only once before dying, indigenous to Haleakala — growing in an enclosure near it. From the summit at Pu'u Ulaula, at an elevation of 10,023 feet, you can gaze down into the mammoth crater — 3,000 feet deep, $7\frac{1}{2}$ miles long and $2\frac{1}{2}$ miles wide — sweeping across a vast lunar landscape. From here, too, you can view the entire island of Maui, as well as the nearby islands of Molokai, Lanai, Kaho'olawe, and even Hawaii, the Big Island, to the south. There are, by the way, two or three trails looping through the crater as well, including the Silversword Loop Trail which — yes, you guessed it — has some silverswords along it; and the Sliding Sands and Halemauu trails, which also journey through the crater. Besides which, there is a visitor center situated on the rim of the crater, quite close to the summit, with exhibits and information on the geology and eruption history of Haleakala.

At any rate, Haleakala is one of Hawaii's great wonders, and among the tallest mountains in the world, with a base some 20,000

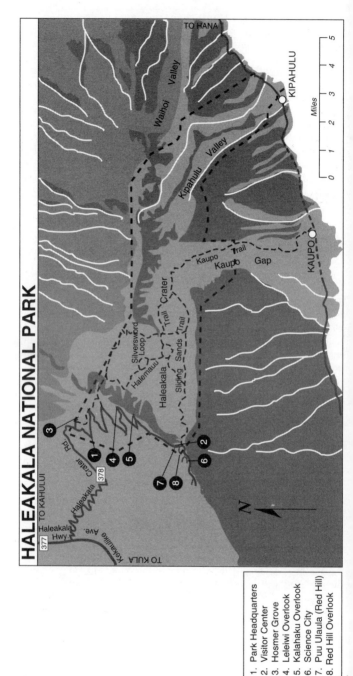

HALEAKALA NATIONAL PARK

TO HANA

Waihoi Valley

KIPAHULU

Kipahulu Valley

KAUPO

Kaupo Trail

Kaupo Gap

Crater Trail

Silversword Loop

Halemauu

Haleakala

Sliding Sands Trail

Miles
0 1 2 3 4 5

Haleakala Crater Rd

378

TO KAHULUI

377 Haleakala Hwy

Kekaulike Ave.

TO KULA

N

1. Park Headquarters
2. Visitor Center
3. Hosmer Grove
4. Leleiwi Overlook
5. Kalahaku Overlook
6. Science City
7. Puu Ulaula (Red Hill)
8. Red Hill Overlook

feet beneath the ocean, and its head more or less perpetually in the clouds, more than 10,000 feet above. It is also a place of immense beauty, and mysticism, and a source of infinite, unharnessed energy. Indeed, novelist Jack London described it in his *House of the Sun* as "a noble dwelling situated on the island of Maui," with "a message of beauty and wonder for the human soul that cannot be delivered by proxy."

Haleakala, we might add, is also a place of spirituality, sacred to Hawaiians, where the *kahunas* — Hawaiian priests — once worshipped, and where, we are told, in times immemorable, demigod Maui, son of goddess Hina, lassoed the sun and forced it to slow its path over the great mountain in order that his mother may dry her *kapa* cloth. According to legend, Maui braided a rope from coconut fiber, tied a noose at one end of it, and lay in wait for the sun in "The House of the Sun"; and as the sun journeyed over the mountain, Maui lassoed the sun's rays, one at a time, and broke them off, until the sun conceded to him. And so, to this day, the sun lingers longer over Haleakala.

The best time to visit Haleakala, of course, especially for first time visitors, is at sunrise — although sunsets can be quite spectacular too — before the morning clouds cover the peak. It is, however, advisable to dress warmly for the morning spectacle, as the temperatures are likely to be at least 30° lower than in the island's lower elevations. It is also a good idea, we might suggest, to call the park before visiting, at 808-572-7749, for a report on weather conditions.

The Haleakala National Park, besides the Haleakala Crater, has one or two other points of interest as well. At the north end of the park, for instance, is the Hosmer Grove, which has in it a variety of trees, including pines, spruce, eucalyptus and firs, all planted, in 1910, by Ralph Hosmer, regarded as "Hawaii's Father of Forestry," and for whom the grove is named. There is, incidentally, a half-mile trail that loops through the grove, and also a campground.

Worth visiting, too, quite close to the Hosmer Grove, is the Park Headquarters-Visitor Center, which has maps and brochures and books on the park's geology, flora and fauna, and where you can also see, outside the center, some *nene* — or Hawaiian Goose — Hawaii's state bird. The *nene*, typically, live in the high country around Haleakala, and were once close to extinction, but now have a stable population, of approximately 150.

Finally, there is Science City, at the south end of the park, past the Haleakala summit, Pu'u Ulaula. Science City is essentially a University of Hawaii research facility — although part of the facility is also used by NASA — devoted to the research of solar and lunar activity. It is, however, generally not open to the public.

THE ROAD TO HANA

The Road to Hana — or the Hana Highway — is one of the most beautiful drives on the islands. It sets out from just outside Kahului and journeys southeast along the coast, some 55 miles, to the quaint little town of Hana. The highway twists and turns madly much of the way — around 617 curves! — passing by lush, verdant valleys and scores of picturesque waterfalls, large and small, and crossing some 56 tiny bridges, mostly one-lane. And while it is possible to drive to Hana in less than two hours, this is one drive, as many will attest, that should be enjoyed — or, perhaps, experienced — at a leisurely pace, for it offers in it some of the most breathtaking valley and ocean views, almost at every turn of the highway, and abundant opportunities for taking dips in the refreshing, cool, emerald pools beneath waterfalls — with picnicking beside them — and rare moments of solitude.

Paia

At the top of the Hana Highway, of course, some 6 miles east of Kahului, lies Paia, a small, quaint town — formerly a sugar plantation camp, established at the turn-of-the-century — filled with a colorful assortment of shops, boutiques and galleries, and a handful of eateries, mostly dating from the late 1960s and early 1970s, when Paia was a sleepy little village, inhabited primarily by hippies. Paia, however, is now famous for its windsurfing, with much of the activity centered at nearby Hookipa Beach, situated 2 miles or so from the center of town, reached on the main highway, the Hana Highway (36), eastward, and where you can watch world-class windsurfers perform 360-degree flips in the waves and otherwise hone their skills. The Hookipa Beach Park, we might add, is also the site of the annual Marui/O'Neill Invitational — with a prize of $180,000 — held in April, as well as several other national and international windsurfing competitions.

Just to the west of Paia, too, a half-mile or so, off the highway, lies the H.P. Baldwin Beach Park, with a long, sandy beach, and quite popular with bodysurfing enthusiasts. The Baldwin Beach, interestingly, was the site of Maui's first bodysurfing competition, held in 1977.

Paia has one or two other points of interest as well. Just to the east of town, for instance, also off the highway, stands the Mantokuji Buddhist Temple, with its ornate trim and landscaped Japanese gardens, overlooking the ocean; and a little to the south of the center of town, about a mile, on Baldwin Avenue — which goes off the highway (36) — you can search out the old, historic Paia Sugar Mill, still in operation, and with the distinction of being the oldest sugar mill, in continuous operation, in Maui. The mill, by the way, was built around the turn-of-the-century, by the Alexander & Baldwin interests, founders, too, of Paia.

Waterfall on the road to Hana

King Protea

Southeast from Paia

Southeast from Paia, some 10 miles, the Hana Highway, 36, becomes Hana Highway, 360, and the "Road to Hana" begins in earnest, with open, blue ocean on one side of it, and lush, green hills and valleys on the other. And 2 miles farther, past the start of Highway 360, the road crosses over a highway bridge, the Hoolawa Bridge, the first of several bridges on the Hana Highway, just to the west of which, a well-worn trail dashes off inland, alongside a stream, a little way, to two successive waterfalls, appropriately named Twin Falls. The first of the two falls lies a mile or so from the highway, with a small pool at the foot of it, well worth stopping at for a dip; and the second, and larger, of the two falls can be reached by following the trail upstream from the little pool, another quarter mile, to a large, natural pool, more secluded than the first, into which the fuller, second waterfall plunges; and here, too, needless to say, you can enjoy the pristine pool, or picnic beside it.

From Twin Falls, it is another mile, approximately, to the tiny village of Huelo, reached on a small side road, the Huelo Road, which goes off the highway, toward the ocean, and where you can search out the old, stone-and-coral Kaulanapueo Church, dating from 1853 and situated on a cliff overlooking the ocean; and southeast from there, another 6 miles or so, is a turnout, unmarked, at the head of the Waikamoi Ridge Trail — a picturesque, mile-long nature trail that leads past a variety of indigenous plants and trees, including eucalyptus, and a bamboo grove, and offers magnificent views, along the way, of the Waikamoi Valley and the coastline below, and good picnicking opportunities, besides.

Farther still, another half mile — just before mile marker 10 — are the Waikamoi Falls, located quite close to the road and easily accessible; and a mile or so from there, southeastward, at mile marker 11, is the bridge over Puohokamoa Stream, from where a short trail dashes off back into the valley, to the picturesque, and more popular, Puohokamoa Falls, where there are some picnic tables and a generous-size, natural pool, ideal for swimming. Also worth investigating, a half mile from the Puohokamoa Falls, are Haipua'ena Falls, more secluded than the Puohokamoa Falls, and also with a small, emerald pool at the foot of the waterfall. The Haipua'ena Falls can be reached by following a little trail, overgrown with wild ginger, that goes off the highway from near the southern end of the one-lane highway bridge.

Another half mile from the Haipua'ena Falls, and we are at the Kaumahina State Wayside Park, which has a picnic area and restroom facilities, and an overlook with superb views of the Honomanu Bay and the rugged coastline farther to the southeast. A little way from the park, too, journeying on the highway toward Hana, you can see, on the inland side, the ancient Honomanu Valley, which has in it towering cliffs and a waterfall or two, but is largely inaccessible.

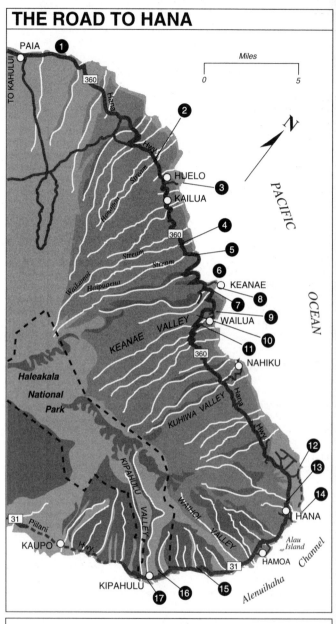

THE ROAD TO HANA

Miles
0 — 5

TO KAHULUI

PAIA ①

360

Hana Hwy

HUELO ③
②

KAILUA ③

360 ④
⑤

⑥
KEANAE ⑧
⑦
⑨ WAILUA
⑩
⑪

KEANAE VALLEY

NAHIKU

360

PACIFIC

OCEAN

Waikamoi
Stream

Honomanu
Stream

Haipuaena
Stream

Haleakala
National
Park

KUHIWA VALLEY

KIPAHULU
VALLEY

WAIHOI
VALLEY

Hana Hwy

⑫ Waianapanapa
⑬
⑭ HANA

Alau
Island

31
Piilani Hwy

KAUPO

31
HAMOA

Channel

⑮
⑯
KIPAHULU
⑰

Alenuihaha

1. Hookipa Beach Park
2. Twin Falls
3. Kaulanapueo Church
4. Waikamoi Ridge Trail
5. Haipuaena Falls
6. Keanae Peninsula
7. Keanae Lookout

8. Ihiihi o Iehowa
   o na Kaua Church
9. St. Gabriel's Church
10. Keanae Valley-
    Wailua Overlook
11. Lookout
12. Waianapanapa
    State Park

13. Helani Gardens
14. Kauiki Head
15. Wailua Falls
16. Oheo Gulch
17. Palapala
    Hoomau Church
    and Lindbergh
    Grave

Ke'anae Peninsula

From the Kaumahina State Wayside Park, it is another 4 miles or so to the beautiful Ke'anae Peninsula, a more or less flat tract of land, jutting out northward into the ocean. But first, before reaching the peninsula, situated alongside the highway itself — a half mile past mile marker 16 — is the Ke'anae Arboretum, where you can view a variety of indigenous Hawaiian plants and trees, including native forest trees, tropical trees introduced to Hawaii, and cultivated Hawaiian plants. There are also, at the arboretum, irrigated patches of *taro*, from the root of which, *poi*, a Hawaiian staple, rich in nutrients, is made; and an authentic representation of a Hawaiian rain forest.

In any event, the Ke'anae Peninsula, quite picturesque with its green, patchwork quilt of *taro*, and originally formed by a lava flow from the Haleakala Crater that passed through the Ko'olau Gap and the Ke'anae Valley on the way to the coast, can be reached on a side road, off the Hana Highway, just past the Ke'anae Arboretum, northeastward. Ke'anae itself is rather serene, and rural, with a handful of small homesteads, surrounded, naturally, by *taro*, and which has in it, of interest to the visitor, the lovely, steepled Lanakila 'ihi'ihi o lehowa o na Kaua Church, built from stone and coral, and dating from 1860. At Ke'anae, too, at the northern tip of the peninsula, you can visit Ke'anae Point, which has superb, commanding views of the ocean.

Also of interest, a half mile from the Ke'anae turnoff, just past mile marker 17, is the Ke'anae Overlook, unmarked, but with stunning, picture-postcard views of the Ke'anae Peninsula; and a little way from there, another half mile or so, is the halfway point to Hana, dotted with a handful of fruit-stands — best known among them the long-established Uncle Harry's — all located alongside the highway, and where you can sample a variety of locally-grown fruit — starfruit, papayas, mountain apples, strawberry guavas.

Wailua to Hana

Southeastward from the halfway mark to Hana, past mile marker 18, the Wailua Road dashes off the highway, toward the ocean, to the little village of Wailua, which has in it not one but two steepled churches — the stone-and-coral St. Gabriel's Church, where services are now held, and the adjacent, surprisingly small, historic Coral Miracle Church, built in 1860, from coral washed onto the Wailua Beach, following a freak storm. There are also some good views from here, looking inland, of the scenic Waikani Falls, cascading more than a hundred feet.

A little farther on, just past mile marker 19, on the *mauka* — inland — side of the highway, is the Ke'anae Valley-Wailua Lookout, which has spectacular views of the lush Ke'anae Valley which extends all the way to Ko'olau Gap, more or less at the rim of the Haleakala crater. At the lookout, too, following the stairs to the right, you can enjoy a splendid view of Wailua directly below.

Farther still is the Pua'aka'a State Wayside Park, situated approximately midway between mile markers 22 and 23 on the Hana Highway. The park has in it one or two small waterfalls, with a delightful little pool and a gushing spring, and some good picnicking possibilities. A short walk from the highway, on the *mauka* side, leads to the falls.

Another 8 miles or so, at mile marker 31, Ulaino Road dashes off from the highway, seaward, one and one-half miles, to Kalahu Point, where you can visit the beautiful Kahanu Gardens, a 126-acre tropical botanical garden, now part of the National Tropical Botanical Garden. The garden grows and displays a collection of ethnobotanical plants — including breadfruit and coconut trees — which have been used by Hawaiians for centuries for their food and medicinal properties, as well as in clothing, baskets and dishes. There is also a visitor's center here, which has guidebooks for the garden, detailing a self-guided walking tour of the grounds.

Also at the garden, of interest to the visitor, is Hawaii's largest *heiau* — or temple — the Pi'ilanihale Heiau, meaning "Home of Pi'ilani" (Pi'ilani, of course, was the first chief of Maui, during the 15th century). The *heiau* stands 50 feet high, overlooking ancient fishponds. It is also, quite interestingly, one of the oldest such relics on the island, dating from 1270 A.D.

Next up, at mile marker 32, is the Wai'anapanapa State Park, lying just two miles north of the town of Hana. Wai'anapanapa, meaning "glistening water," derives its name from a large lava-tube cave located in the park, reached by way of a well-marked trail that starts out at the northeast end of the parking area, and which has in it some natural pools with good swimming possibilities. The cave, interestingly, is also intertwined with a local legend, which endures that Maui's Chief Kaakea once suspected his wife, Popoalaea, of infidelity, thus invoking his wrath. Popoalaea, needless to say, fled from her husband, and hid in this cave where, eventually, Kaakea found her and killed her. On certain nights, we are told, the pools in the cave turn a murky red from the blood of the slain Princess Popoalaea — a grim reminder of the infamous event. (In reality, however, it is the thousands of tiny red shrimp that fill the pools occasionally that give them the bloody red effect.)

In any case, the Wai'anapanapa State Park has a lovely picnic area, directly above a small, black-sand beach, and camping facilities as well as rental cabins. It also has, at the front of the picnic area, a natural rock arch, which adds to the interest. Swimming, however, is not encouraged at the beach, due to the fact that the bay is largely unprotected, making it rather unsafe for the sport. From Wai'anapanpa, too, an old Hawaiian trail leads to Hana, journeying along the coastline for the most part, passing by growths of *hala*, ancient burial sites, and some *heiaus*.

Also worth visiting, just out from Hana, roughly a mile past the Wai'anapanapa State Park, are the Helani Gardens — a lovely, 70-acre, drive-through botanical garden, filled with lavish displays of Hawaiian plantlife. The garden offers picnicking and walking possibilities.

From the Helani Gardens, of course, it is another mile, approximately, south on the Hana Highway, to Hana, our main destination.

Hana

Hana, frequently romanticized as "Heavenly Hana," and situated at the head of Hana Bay, at the eastern end of the island, is a surprising little town, rural, secluded, tranquil, unpretentious, and largely unchanged in more than a hundred years. It is also, we might add, an historic town, originally founded as a sugar plantation town — one of the earliest on the island — in 1864, and where sugar remained the principal industry until the early 1930s, bringing to the area hundreds of Chinese, Japanese and Portuguese plantation workers, whose descendants — together with several full-blooded Hawaiians — continue to make up a large part of Hana's resident population, of around 1,000.

In any event, Hana, it must be right to say, is really quite easy to explore, with only a half-dozen or so streets, all told. At the heart of it are the Hotel Hana-Maui and Hana Ranch, the latter established in the 1940s by Paul Fagan, a San Francisco millionaire, who purchased, in 1943, some 14,000 acres of prime sugarcane land in and around Hana, following the collapse of the sugar industry, and converted the cane fields into ranch land. The Hana Ranch — which, along with the Hotel Hana-Maui, is the chief employer in the Hana area — is now a working ranch of sorts, encompassing some 4,500 acres on the outskirts of town, and where guests of the Hotel Hana-Maui can enjoy horseback and hay-wagon rides, among other outdoor pursuits. The ranch, however, for the most part, is not open to the general public.

The Hotel Hana-Maui, of course, quite possibly *the* centerpiece of Hana, and also built by Paul Fagan, in 1947, as the Hotel Hana Ranch — an exclusive resort for his well-heeled guests — is situated more or less at the center of town, just off the Hana Highway, between Keawa Place and Hauoli Street. The hotel itself, which boasts among its guests such celebrities as bestselling author James Michener and former Beatle George Harrison, consists of 12 rather simple, single-story bungalow-style buildings (housing 97 guest rooms and suites, in all), with thatched roofs — luxury accommodations, no less! — tucked away among palms, fruit trees, ferns and other native plants and flowers, on a 23-acre site. The hotel also features an open lobby — yes, with a thatched roof, too — and two well-appointed restaurants — with hula shows featured at one of them, on certain nights of the week — as well as a fresh-water swimming pool, tennis courts, and a small, 3-hole golf course. Besides which, there is a sandy beach just to the south of here, with excellent swimming and sunbathing possibilities, where the hotel staff organizes activities and catered meals for the guests, including traditional Hawaiian luaus.

Also of interest, directly across from the Hotel Hana-Maui, on

HANA

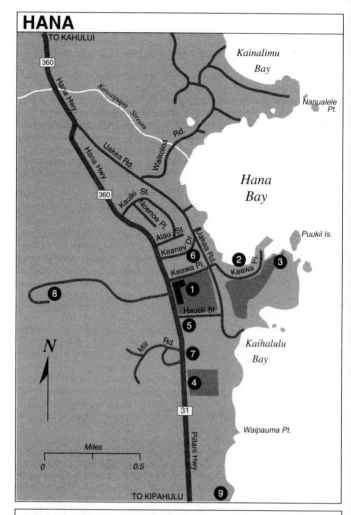

1. Hotel Hana Maui
2. Hana Beach Park
3. Kauiki Head
4. Hana Hongwanji Buddhist Temple
5. Wananalua Church
6. Hana Cultural Center
7. Hasegawa Store
8. Fagan Memorial Beach
9. Hamoa Beach

Lyon's Hill, stands a large lava-stone cross, built as a memorial to Paul Fagan, following his death in 1959. From the top of the hill, too, you can enjoy some good views, of the ocean and Hana Bay, and the Hana township below.

Among other places worth visiting here, are the Wananalua Church, dating from 1838 and built from coral blocks, located adjacent to the Hotel Hana-Maui on the Hana Highway; the Hana Cultural Center, located on Uakea Road, just to the north of Keawa Place, which has in it a small museum displaying various Hawaiian artifacts, such as quilts, bowls and historic photographs, and where you can also visit the old courthouse and jail cells; and the famous Hasegawa Store, quite possibly Hana's foremost tourist attraction, which burnt down in August, 1990, and was subsequently relocated at its present address, at 5165 Hana Highway. This last, the Hasegawa Store, is much to be recommended to visitors to Hana — an historic, family-run general store, piled high with almost every imaginable item — from groceries to lawn-mowers to stereo systems — and immortalized in song and visited, over the years, by a host of celebrities — Kris Kristofferson, Jim Nabors, Steve Forrest, Richard Pryor, Carol Burnett, Burt Reynolds and George Harrison, among others.

Try to also visit the glorious Hana Bay at the east end of town, along the southern shore of which, reached more or less directly on Keawa Place — which goes off the Hana Highway, passing through the center of town — is the Hana Beach Park, with a sandy beach with good swimming possibilities, and a popular little eatery, Tutu's, one of only three eating establishments in Hana. Just to the east of the beach, too, at the southeastern corner of Hana Bay rises Kauiki Head, a 386-foot-high, red cinder cone, site of several pitched battles for the defense of the island, and where, in fact, in 1780, Maui's King Kahekili successfully repelled an onslaught from Hawaii's King Kalaniopuu — one of the most famous of the battles fought here. Kauiki Head, we might add, is also notable as the birthplace of Queen Ka'ahumanu, the favorite wife of King Kamehameha I, who was instrumental in breaking down the ancient Hawaiian *kapu* system, by persuading Kamehameha II to eat a meal, at the same table, with women.

South from Hana the Hana Highway becomes the Pi'ilani Highway (31), and strung along it, just out from town, are two delightful beaches. The first of these, the Koki Beach Park, is located a little over a mile from town, along Haneoo Road, which goes off the highway. It is a popular surfing and bodysurfing beach, lined, along its upper slope, with ironwood trees. Just offshore from here, you can see Alau Island, a seabird sanctuary, and a little to the south, a mile or so, and also along Haneoo Road, lies Hamoa Beach, used by Hotel Hana-Maui guests. The Hamoa Beach, however, is also a public beach, and has good swimming and bodysurfing possibilities

South from Hana, too, the Pi'ilani Highway becomes narrower, and serpentine, weaving madly around hairpin bends and treating the motorist to some spectacular coastal scenery much of the way. At Wailua, of course, some 7 miles south of Hana, you can view the picturesque, 95-foot Wailua Falls, and 3 miles farther lies the wild, lush Oheo — or "Seven Sacred Pools" — Gulch, at the ocean end of the Kipahulu Valley, comprising the southeastern corner of the Haleakala National Park, and with the Paukea Stream meandering through the midst of it. Oheo, the name, however, it must be fair to say, is rather misleading, for the area has in it not seven but well over 20 natural pools — most with some swimming possibilities — and the pools, we are told, are in no way sacred. In any case, the gulch has a fair number of waterfalls as well, small and large, and a handful of scenic hiking trails, including a half-mile loop that leads to a series of lower pools, closer to, and overlooking, the ocean, and a 2-mile trail that journeys to the Waimoku Falls, farther back in the gulch, passing by, along the way, the Makahiku Falls, and crossing one or two streams and winding through some astonishing bamboo forests, besides. The Oheo Gulch, we might add, also offers good views of the ocean and the Big Island of Hawaii to the south, and has in it, in addition, a ranger station, where you can obtain weather and other information before venturing into the gulch.

From the Oheo Gulch, it is roughly a mile, on the Pi'ilani Highway, to Kipahulu, a tiny village, which has in it the historic Palapala Ho'omau Church, dating from 1857, and a small, seaside cemetery adjacent to the church, where you can search out the grave of pioneer aviator Charles A. Lindbergh, buried here in 1974. Also near the church is the Kipahulu Point Park, comprising a small, grassy area, situated atop Kipahulu Point, overlooking the ocean. The park also has good picnicking possibilities.

Beyond Kipahulu, of course, a mile or so, the paved road ends, and not until 7½ miles farther, past the village of Kaupo, does it begin again.

PRACTICAL INFORMATION FOR MAUI

HOW TO GET THERE

Maui is situated approximately 35 miles northwest of the Big Island of Hawaii, with Molokai and Lanai to its north and west, respectively, each some 9 miles distant, and with Oahu 75 miles to the northwest. It can be reached directly from the U.S. mainland on regularly scheduled flights, or by way of Honolulu, Oahu, which is serviced by several different domestic as well as international airlines. Commercial flights arrive and depart at Maui's *Kahului Airport*; commuter flights, between Honolulu and Maui are also available to and from the island's *Kapalua Airport*, located near the

Kapalua Resort in West Maui, just north of Ka'anapali, and the *Hana Airport*, located at Hana, on Maui's east shore.

Direct to Maui

Direct flights from the U.S. mainland to Maui are available on *Delta Air Lines* (800) 221-1212 and *United Airlines* (800) 241-6522. For schedules and fare information, contact the respective airlines.

Via Honolulu

Domestic Airlines. The following domestic airlines service the Honolulu Airport: *American Airlines* (800) 433-7300; *America West* (800) 247-5692; *Delta Air Lines* (800) 221-1212; *Hawaiian Airlines* (800) 882-8811; *Northwest Airlines* (800) 225-2525; and *United Airlines* (800) 241-6522.

International Airlines. The following international airlines offer scheduled flights to Honolulu: *Air New Zealand* (800) 262-1234; *Canadian Airlines International* (800) 426-7000; *China Airlines* (808) 536-6951; *Japan Air Lines* (800) 232-2517; *Korea Air* (808) 923-7302; *Philippines Airlines* (800) 435-9725; and *Singapore Airlines* (808) 542-6063.

Honolulu to Maui

The following airlines offer regular, scheduled inter-island flights between Honolulu, Oahu, and Maui: *Aloha Airlines* (808) 244-9071/(800) 367-5250; *Island Air* (800) 652-6541/(800) 323-3345; and *Hawaiian Airlines* (808) 871-6132/(800) 367-5320. Fares, typically, range from $49-$99 one-way, to $98-$138 round-trip. Multi-day, unlimited travel passes are also available.

Inter-island Flights

Flights are also available between Maui and the nearby islands of Molokai and Lanai. The following airlines offer services between the islands: *Air Molokai* (808) 877-0026; *Aloha Airlines* (808) 224-9071/(800) 367-5250; *Island Air* (800) 652-6541/(800) 323-3345; and *Hawaiian Airlines* (800) 367-5320.

Inter-island Ferries

There are, in addition to inter-island flights, daily ferry services available between Maui and the islands of Molokai and Lanai. Ferry boats shuttle between Lahaina, West Maui, and Kaunakakai, Molokai, and Manele Bay, Lanai. The fare for adults, from Maui to either of the islands, Molokai or Lanai, is $25.00 one-way. For ferry services to Molokai, contact *Maui Princess,* 505 Front St., Room 225, Lahaina, (808) 661-8397/(800) 833-5800; for services to Lanai, contact *Expeditions on Maui,* Lahaina, (808) 661-3756.

TOURIST INFORMATION

Hawaii Visitors Bureau (HVB) - Maui. 250 Alamaha St., Kahului, HI 96733; (808) 871-8691/(800) 525-MAUI. Wealth of tourist information available, including directory of accommodations and restaurants and a calendar of events. Also maps, and a tourist publication, *The Islands of Hawaii: A Vacation Planner*, covering places of interest on the islands, recreation and tours. The *Hawaii Visitors Bureau* also maintains offices at the following locations: *HVB Main Office,* Waikiki Business Plaza, 2270 Kalakaua Ave., Suite 808, Honolulu, HI 96815, (808) 923-1811; *HVB Los Angeles,* 3440 Wilshire Blvd., Suite 502, CA 90010, (213) 385-5301; *HVB San Francisco,* 50 California St., Suite 450, San Francisco, CA 94111, (415) 392-8173.

Maui Chamber of Commerce. 26 N. Pu'unene Ave., Kahului, HI 96733; (808) 871-7711. Visitor information brochures, including lodging, restaurant and tour company listings.

Publications. There are also several free publications available on the island, at airports, hotels, restaurants and shopping centers, with valuable tourist information and articles of local interest. The following are among the best-known — the *Drive Guide*, published three times a year and available at rental car agencies, offers information on dining, island activities and sightseeing, and includes maps; *Maui Beach Press*, published weekly on Mondays, features up-to-date information on dining, entertainment, activities and island adventures, and also contains an island map and discount coupons; *Guide to Maui*, a monthly magazine, offers tips on dining, shopping, fun activities and sightseeing, with maps and coupons; *Maui Gold*, published quarterly, contains directory listings, maps and coupons; and *This Week Maui*, a weekly magazine, contains information on activities on the island, and shopping, dining and sightseeing, as well as maps and discount coupons.

HOW TO GET AROUND

By Car. Rental cars are available from several different car rental agencies on the island. Rental rates for sub-compacts to larger luxury cars range from $18-$70 per day to $180-$320 per week. Some of the companies also offer four-wheel-drive vehicles, especially useful if you plan to visit some of the more remote parts of the island. For rentals, availability and more information, contact any of the following: *Alamo,* Kahului Airport, (800) 327-9633; *Avis,* Kahului Airport, (800) 831-8000; *Budget,* Kahului Airport, (800) 527-0700; *Dollar,* Kahului Airport, (800) 800-4000; *Hertz,* Kahului Airport, (800) 654-3011; *National,* (800) 227-7368; *Andres,* Kahului Airport, (808) 877-5378; *Thrifty,* Kahului Airport, (808) 871-7596/(800) 367-2277; *Kihei Rent-A-Car,* Kihei, (808) 879-7257; *Adventure Rent A Jeep,* 571 Haleakala Hwy., Kahului, (808) 877-6626; or *V.I.P. Car Rentals,* (800) 367-6080/(808) 877-2054.

By Taxi. The following taxi companies service the island: *Ka'anapali*

Taxi, (808) 661-5285/877-5244; *Kihei Taxi,* (808) 879-3000; *Sunshine Cabs,* (808) 879-2220/667-2220; *Wailea Taxi,* (808) 874-5000; and *Yellow Cab of Maui,* (808) 877-7000. Taxi fares from the Kahului Airport, typically, are $40 to the Ka'anapali area and $18 to Kihei.

By Shuttle Bus. Shuttle bus services are available between the Kahului Airport and Ka'anapali Beach Resort and the Kihei-Makena area, as well as between Ka'anapali and the West Maui airport at Kapalua and between the Ka'anapali Resort and the Wharf Shopping Center. Fares from the Kahului Airport to Kihei-Makena are around $10.00, and from the airport to Ka'anapali, $13.00; shuttle services between Ka'anapali and Kapalua and Ka'anapali and the Wharf Shopping Center are free. For schedules and more information, contact any of the following shuttle bus companies: *Akina,* (808) 879-2828; *Trans Hawaiian Maui,* (808) 877-7308; *Maui Express Shuttle,* (808) 874-6210, *Ka'anapali Beach Resort Shuttle,* (808) 667-7411; *The Cannery Shuttle,* (808) 661-5304; or *The Wharf Shuttle,* (808) 661-8748.

ACCOMMODATIONS

Lahaina and Ka'anapali

Aston Ka'anapali Shores. *$119-$395.* 3445 Honoapi'ilani Hwy., Ka'anapali; (808) 667-2211/(800) 922-7866/(800) 321-2558 in Hawaii. 427 oceanfront condominium units, with TV, phones, air-conditioning, and kitchen facilities. Swimming pool, tennis court, restaurant and cocktail lounge, meeting rooms, shops. Daily maid service.

The Coconut Inn. *$75-$95.* 181 Hui Rd., F, Napili; (808) 669-5712. 49-unit condominium complex, located near the beach. TV, phones, and full kitchens. Also swimming pool and spa, and complimentary continental breakfast. Maid service. Handicapped facilities. Minimum stay: 2 days.

Colony's Napili Shores. *$165-$190.* 5351 Lower Honoapi'ilani Hwy., Napili; (808) 669-8061/(800) 777-1700. 114 condominium units, on Napili Beach. TV, phones, and kitchens. Swimming pools, jacuzzi, restaurant and cocktail lounge, and shop on premises. Maid service.

Embassy Suites Resort. *$210-$450.* 104 Ka'anapali Shores Place, Honokowai; (808) 661-2000/(800) 462-6284. 413-unit resort, located on the beach. TV, phones, mini kitchens, and air-conditioning. Swimming pool, health club, spa; restaurant and cocktail lounge; meeting rooms, shops. Handicapped facilities.

Hale Kai Condominiums. *$80-$110.* 3691 Lower Honoapi'ilani Hwy., Honokowai; (808) 669-6333/(800) 446-7307. 40 oceanfront condominium units, with TV, phones, ceiling fans and kitchenettes. Swimming pool. Maid service. Minimum stay: 3 days.

Hyatt Regency Maui. *$230-$430.* 200 Nohea Kai Dr., Ka'anapali; (808) 661-1234/(800) 233-1234. 815-room luxury resort hotel. Facilities include swimming pools, health club and spa, tennis courts, golf course, restaurants and cocktail lounges, meeting rooms, and shops and beauty salon. Handicapped facilities.

Ka'anapali Ali'i. *$195-$450.* 50 Nohea Kai Dr., Ka'anapali; (808) 667-1400/(800) 642-MAUI. 210 oceanfront condominium units, with TV, phones, air-conditioning, and kitchens. Also swimming pool, health club and spa, and tennis courts. Daily maid service. Minimum stay, 3 days.

Ka'anapali Beach Hotel. *$119-$525.* 2525 Ka'anapali Pkwy., Ka'anapali; (808) 661-0011/(800) 262-8450. Beachfront hotel with 430 units with TV, phones, and air-conditioning. Swimming pool, restaurants and cocktail lounge, meeting rooms, shops and beauty salon. Handicapped facilities.

Ka'anapali Royal. *$150-$220.* 2560 Kekaa Dr., Ka'anapali; (808) 661-4804/(800) 367-7040. 105 condominium units, with TV, phones, kitchen facilities, air-conditioning, and daily maid service. Swimming pool, tennis courts, golf course. Handicapped facilities. Minimum stay, 2 nights.

Kahana Sunset. *$135-$165.* 4909 Lower Honoapi'ilani Hwy., Kahana; (808) 669-8011/(800) 669-1488. 71 condominium units on the beach. TV, phones, kitchens; also swimming pool. Daily maid service. Minimum stay, 3 days.

Kahana Villa. *$100-$205.* 4242 Lower Honoapi'ilani Hwy., Kahana; (808) 669-5613/(808) 992-9700. 100 condominium units, with phones and kitchens. Swimming pool, tennis court, restaurant and cocktail lounge. Maid service.

Kahili Maui. *$80-$130.* 5500 Honoapi'ilani Rd., Kapalua; (808) 786-7387/(800) SUNSETS. 30 condominium units; TV, phones, kitchens, and maid service. Swimming pool. Located directly across the street from beach.

Kapalua Bay Hotel & Villas. *$225-$485.* One Bay Dr., Kapalua; (808) 669-5656/(800) 367-8000. Luxury, oceanfront resort, with 319 oceanview rooms and suites, situated on 750 acres. Facilities include swimming pools, tennis courts, golf courses, restaurants and cocktail lounge, shops, and beauty salon. Handicapped facilities.

Kulakane. *$90-$135.* 3741 Lower Honoapi'ilani Rd., Honokowai; (808) 669-6119/(800) 367-6088. 42 condominium units with ocean views; TV, phones, kitchens, maid service. Swimming pool. Minimum stay: 3 days.

Lahaina Shores Beach Resort. *$95-$225.* 475 Front St., Lahaina; (808) 661-4835/(800) 628-6699. 199-unit beachfront resort. TV, phones, kitchens, and air-conditioning. Swimming pool. Daily maid service. Handicapped facilities.

Mahana at Ka'anapali. *$105-$300.* 110 Ka'anapali Shore Pl., Ka'anapali; (808) 661-8751/(800) 922-7866/(800) 321-2558 in Hawaii. 215 oceanview condominium units, with TV and phones, air-conditioning, and full kitchens. Swimming pool, tennis courts. Handicapped facilities, Minimum stay: 3 days.

Maui Eldorado Resort. *$99-$295.* 2661 Kekaa Dr., Ka'anapali; (808) 922-9700/(800) 535-0085/(800) 219-9700 in Hawaii. 204 oceanfront condominium units, with TV, phones, air-conditioning, kitchens, and washer and dryer. Swimming pool and shops on premises. Daily maid service.

Maui Islander Hotel. *$69-$104.* 660 Wainee St., Lahaina; (808) 667-9766/(800) 367-5226/(800) 542-6827 in Hawaii. 360 units, with TV, phones, and air-conditioning; some kitchen facilities. Swimming pool, tennis court. Handicapped facilities.

Maui Ka'anapali Villas. *$99-$250.* 45 Kai Ala Dr., Ka'anapali; (808) 667-7791/(800) 922-7866/(800) 321-2558 in Hawaii. Beachfront condominium complex with 250 units. TV, phones, air-conditioning, kitchens. Also swimming pool and shops on premises. Maid service. Handicapped facilities.

Maui Marriott. *$195-$400.* 100 Nohea Kai Dr., Ka'anapali; (808) 667-1200/(800) 228-9290. 720-room full-service resort hotel, located on Ka'anapali Beach. Hotel facilities include swimming pools, health club, tennis courts, golf courses, restaurants and cocktail lounge, shops, and beauty salon. Handicapped facilities.

Maui Park. *$79-$159.* 3626 Lower Honoapi'ilani Hwy., Honokowai; (808) 669-6622/(800) 922-7866/(800) 321-2558 in Hawaii. 288 condominium units, with TV, phones, ceiling fans, kitchens, and maid service. Swimming pool. Handicapped facilities.

Mauian Hotel. *$70-$150.* 5441 Honoapi'ilani Rd., Napili; (808) 669-6205/(800) 367-5034. 44 studio apartments, fronting on Napili Bay. TV and phones; kitchens, ceiling fans. Swimming pool and meeting rooms.

Napili Kai Beach Club. *$165-$400.* 5900 Honoapi'ilani Rd., Napili; (808) 669-6271/(800) 367-5030. 165-unit condominium complex, located on Napili Bay. TV, phones, kitchens; swimming pools, tennis courts, restaurant and cocktail lounge, and shops. Handicapped facilities.

Napili Point Resort. *$134-$235.* 5295 Honoapi'ilani Hwy., Napili; (808) 669-9222/(800) 669-6252. 115 oceanfront condominium units, with TV, phones, and kitchens. Swimming pools. Daily maid service.

Napili Sunset. *$75-$100.* 46 Hui Dr., Napili; (808) 669-8083/(800) 447-9229. Beachfront condominium complex with 42 units with TV and phones. Swimming pool. Maid service. Minimum stay, 3 days.

Napili Surf Beach Resort. *$95-$155.* 50 Napili Pl., Napili; (808) 669-8002/(800) 541-0638. 54 beachfront condominium units, with TV, and kitchens. Swimming pools; maid service. Minimum stay: 5 days.

Napili Village. *$79-$97.* 5425 Lower Honoapi'ilani Hwy., Napili; (808) 669-6228/(800) 336-2185. 30 condominium units, with TV and kitchens. Swimming pool, beauty salon, and shops. Short walk to beach. Minimum stay: 3 days.

Noelani Condominium Resort. *$87-$170.* 4095 Lower Honoapi'ilani Rd., Kahana; (808) 669-8374/(800) 367-6030. 50 units in oceanfront condominium complex. TV, phones, and kitchens. Swimming pools. Minimum stay: 3 days.

Pioneer Inn. *$32-$80.* 658 Wharf St., Lahaina; (808) 661-3636/(800) 457-5457. 48 rooms in historic inn, built in 1901. Restaurant and bar on premises, with live entertainment. Located in the center of town.

Plantation Inn. *$99-$179.* 174 Lahainaluna Rd., Lahaina; (808) 667-9225/(800) 433-6815. Country-style inn with 18 units; TV, phones, air-conditioning. Swimming pool, restaurants and cocktail lounge. Maid service. Minimum stay: 3 days.

Polynesian Shores. *$110-$165.* 3975 Lower Honoapi'ilani Hwy., Honokowai; (808) 669-6065/(800) 433-6284. 52 oceanfront condominium units, with TV, phones, and full kitchens. Swimming pool. Minimum stay, 3 days.

Ritz Carlton. *$285-$2,800.* 1 Ritz Carlton Dr., Kapalua; (808) 669-6200/(800) 241-3333. 550-room luxury resort hotel. Facilities include a swimming pool, health club, spa, golf course and tennis courts; also restaurants and cocktail lounge.

Royal Lahaina Resort. *$145-$295.* 2780 Kekaa Dr., Ka'anapali; (808) 661-3611/(800) 447-6925. Beachfront hotel with 592 units. TV, phones, some kitchens. Swimming pools, tennis courts and golf course. Restaurant and cocktail lounge, meeting rooms, and shops and beauty salon on premises. Handicapped facilities.

Sands of Kahana. *$185-$335.* 4299 Lower Honoapi'ilani Rd., Kahana; (808) 669-0400/(800) 367-7052. 196 beachfront condominium units, with TV, phones, and kitchens. Swimming pool, health club with spa, and restaurants and cocktail lounge.

Sheraton Maui Hotel. *$495-$300.* 2605 Ka'anapali Pkwy., Ka'anapali; (808) 661-0031/(800) 325-3535. 492-room full-service resort hotel, situated on Ka'anapali Beach. Facilities include swimming pool, tennis courts, golf course, restaurant and cocktail lounge, meeting rooms, and shops. Handicapped facilities.

The Westin Maui. *$210-$395.* 2365 Ka'anapali Pkwy., Ka'anapali; (808) 667-2525/(800) 228-3000. Luxury resort hotel with 761 rooms and suites, fronting on Ka'anapali Beach. Hotel facilities include swimming pools, health club and spa, restaurants and cocktail lounges, shops and beauty salon. Handicapped facilities.

The Whaler on Ka'anapali Beach. *$175-$340.* 2481 Ka'anapali Pkwy., Ka'anapali; (808) 661-4861/(800) 367-7052. 340-unit beachfront resort. TV and phones, air-conditioning, kitchens. Swimming pool, health club and spa, and meeting rooms. Daily maid service. Handicapped facilities.

Kihei - Makena

Aston Kamaole Sands. *$95-$275.* 2695 S. Kihei Rd., Kihei; (808) 874-8700/(800) 922-7866/(800) 321-2558 in Hawaii. 345 condominium units, with TV, phones, air-conditioning, and kitchens. Swimming pool, tennis court and restaurant on premises. Daily maid service. Limited wheelchair access.

Four Seasons Resort Wailea. *$350-$1,500.* 3900 Wailea Alanui, Wailea; (808) 874-8000/(800) 334-MAUI/(800) 332-3442. 380-room luxury resort, overlooking Wailea Beach. Facilities include a swimming pool, health club with spa, tennis courts, restaurants and cocktail lounge, meeting rooms, and shops.

Grand Champions Village. *$160-$230.* 3750 Wailea Alanui Dr., Wailea; (808) 879-1595/(800) 367-5246. 25-unit condominium complex, situated on the Wailea Blue Golf Course. TV, phones, air-conditioning; swimming pool, tennis court and golf facilities. Restaurant and cocktail lounge. Daily maid service. Minimum stay: 3 days.

Grand Wailea Resort, Hotel & Spa. *$350-$2,000.* 3850 Wailea Alanui, Wailea; (808) 875-1234/(800) 223-6800/(800) 888-6100. Luxury, oceanfront resort hotel, with 787 rooms and suites. Hotel facilities include swimming pools, health club and spa, tennis courts, golf course, restaurants, shops and beauty salon. Handicapped facilities.

Hale Pau Hana Resort. *$155-$190.* 2480 S. Kihei Rd., Kihei; (808) 879-2715/(800) 367-6036. 80 oceanfront condominium units, with TV, phones, and kitchens. Swimming pool. Handicapped facilities. Minimum stay: 5 days.

Kamaole Beach Royale Resort. *$90-$185.* 2385 S. Kihei Rd., Kihei; (808) 879-3131/(800) 421-3661. 65 condominium units with TV, phones and kitchens. Swimming pool, meeting rooms. Maid service. Handicapped facilities. Located directly across from beach. Minimum stay: 5 days.

Kea Lani Hotel. *$235-$995.* 4100 Wailea Alanui, Wailea; (808)875-4100/(800)882-4100. 450 rooms and suites in luxury beachfront hotel. TV, phones, stereos, and kitchenettes. Swimming pool, health club and spa, restaurants, cocktail lounge, meeting rooms, shops and beauty salon.

Kihei Bay Vista. *$95-$110.* 679 S. Kihei Rd., Kihei; (808) 879-8866/(800) 367-7040. 60 condominium units; TV, phones, air-conditioning, kitchens. Swimming pool on premises. Daily maid service. Minimum stay, 2 days.

Kihei Beach Resort. *$110-$145.* 36 S. Kihei Rd., Kihei; (808) 879-2744/(800) 367-6034. 34 beachfront condominium units, with TV, phones and air-conditioning. Swimming pool. Maid service. Handicapped facilities. Minimum stay: 3 days.

Kihei Kai. *$55-$95.* 61 N. Kihei Rd., Kihei; (808) 879-2357/(800) 735-2357. 24 condominium units, with TV, air-conditioning, and kitchens. Swimming pool. Minimum stay: 4 days.

Kihei Surfside Condominium. *$125-$160.* 2936 S. Kihei Rd., Kihei; (808) 879-1488/(800) 367-5240. 83-unit oceanfront condominium complex. TV, phones, full kitchens; also swimming pool. Handicapped facilities. Minimum stay, 3 days.

Lihi Kai Cottages. *$54-$59.* 2121 Iliili Rd., Kihei; (808) 879-2335/(800) 544-4524. 9 oceanfront cottages, with kitchens, and TV. Maid service. Handicapped facilities. Minimum stay, 3 days.

Luana Kai Resort. *$130-$225.* 940 S. Kihei Rd., Kihei; (808) 879-1268/(800) 669-1127. 113 units in oceanfront condominium complex; TV, phones, kitchens. Swimming pool, health club and spa, tennis court. Handicapped facilities. Minimum stay, 3 days.

Makena Surf. *$250-$350.* 3750 Wailea Alanui Dr., Wailea; (808) 879-1595/(800) 367-5246. 25 oceanfront condominium units, with TV, phones, air-conditioning, and kitchens, Swimming pool, golf course, restaurant and cocktail lounge, shops. Maid service. Minimum stay: 3 days.

Mana Kai Maui Resort. *$90-$195.* 2960 S. Kihei Rd., Kihei; (808) 879-1561/(800) 525-2025. Beachfront resort with 98 units with TV and phones; also some kitchen units. Swimming pool, restaurant and cocktail lounge, meeting rooms, shops and beauty salon. Maid service. Handicapped facilities.

Maui Coast Hotel. *$120-$250.* 2259 S. Kihei, Kihei; (808) 874-MAUI/(800) 426-0670. 261-room oceanfront hotel; TV, phones, air-conditioning. Swimming pool, tennis courts, restaurant and cocktail lounge, meeting rooms, and shops on premises. Handicapped facilities.

Maui Hill. *$135-$165.* 2881 S. Kihei Rd., Kihei; (808) 879-6321/879-7751/(800) 922-7866. 42 condominium units, with TV, phones, air-conditioning, and kitchens. Swimming pool, tennis court. Maid service. Handicapped facilities.

Maui Inter-Continental Resort. *$149-$1,425.* 3700 Wailea Alanui Dr., Wailea; (808) 879-1922/(800) 367-2960. Oceanfront, luxury resort hotel, with 516 rooms and suites. Facilities include swimming pools, tennis courts, golf course, restaurant and cocktail lounge, meeting rooms, shops and beauty salon. Handicapped facilities.

Maui Isana Resort. *$110-$140.* 515 S. Kihei Rd., Kihei; (808) 879-7800/(800) 633-3833/(800) 848-7588 in Hawaii. 50 condominium units, with TV, phones, ceiling fans, and kitchens. Swimming pool, restaurant and cocktail lounge, and shops. Daily maid service.

Maui Lu Resort. *$80-$150.* 575 S. Kihei Rd., Kihei; (808) 879-5881/(800) 922-7866/(800) 321-2558. Beachfront resort with 160 units with TV, phones, and air-conditioning. Swimming pool, tennis court, restaurant and cocktail lounge and shop on premises. Maid service.

Maui Prince Hotel. *$220-$820.* 5400 Makena Alanui, Makena; (808) 874-1111/(800) 321-6284. 310-room full-service hotel, fronting on the ocean. Hotel facilities include a swimming pool, tennis courts, golf course, restaurants, cocktail lounge, and meeting rooms. Handicapped facilities.

Maui Schooner Resort. *$125-$175.* 980 S. Kihei Rd., Kihei; (808) 879-5247/(800) 877-7976. 47 units in oceanfront resort. TV, phones, and kitchens; also swimming pool, jacuzzi, spa, and tennis court. Handicapped facilities.

Maui Vista. *$95-$160.* 2191 S. Kihei Rd., Kihei; (808) 879-7966/(800) 922-7866/(800) 321-2558. 279 condominium units, with TV, phones, air-conditioning, and kitchens. Also swimming pool and tennis court on premises. Maid service.

Nani Kai Hale. *$70-$125.* 73 N. Kihei Rd., Kihei; (808) 879-9120/(800) 367-6032. Beachfront condominium complex with 30 units with TV, phones and kitchens. Swimming pool. Maid service. Handicapped facilities. Minimum stay: 3 days.

The Palms at Wailea. *$155-$225.* 3200 Wailea Alanui, Wailea; (808) 879-5800/(800) 367-7040. 150 condominium units; TV, phones, air-conditioning, and kitchens. Swimming pool and health club and spa. Maid service. Handicapped facilities.

Polo Beach Club. *$225-$285.* 3750 Wailea Alanui Dr., Wailea; (808) 879-1595/879-8847/(800) 367-5246. Oceanfront condominium complex, with 30 units with TV, phones, kitchens, air-conditioning, and maid service. Swimming pool, golf course, tennis court. Restaurant and cocktail lounge, meeting rooms, shops. Minimum stay: 3 days.

Shores of Maui. *$90-$115.* 2075 S. Kihei Rd., Kihei; (808) 879-9140/(800) 367-8002. 50 oceanfront condominium units, with TV and air-conditioning. Swimming pool. Minimum stay: 3 days.

Stouffer's Wailea Beach Resort. *$255-$465.* 3550 Wailea Alanui, Wailea; (808) 879-4900/(800) 9-WAILEA. 347-unit luxury resort hotel, situated on the beach. TV, phones; swimming pool, tennis court, restaurant and cocktail lounge, meeting rooms, shops and beauty salon. Handicapped facilities.

Wailea Ekahi Village. *$120-$220.* 3750 Wailea Alanui Dr., Wailea; (808) 879-9272/(800) 367-2954. 295 oceanfront condominium units, with TV, phones, and kitchens; also swimming pool, tennis court, golf course, restaurant and cocktail lounge, and shops. Daily maid service. Minimum stay, 5 days.

Wailea Ekolu Village. *$135-$160.* 3750 Wailea Alanui Dr., Wailea; (808) 879-1595/(800) 367-5246. 30-unit condominium complex, situated on the golf course. TV, phones, kitchens; ocean views. Swimming pool, tennis court, golf facilities, restaurant and cocktail lounge, and shops. Maid service. Minimum stay, 3 days.

Wailea Elua Village. *$165-$300.* 3750 Wailea Alanui Dr., Wailea; (808) 879-1595/(800) 367-5246. 50 oceanfront condominium units, with TV, phones, and kitchens. Also swimming pool, tennis court, golf course, restaurant and cocktail lounge, and shops. Daily maid service. Minimum stay, 3 days.

Kahului - Wailuku

Maui Beach Hotel. *$75-$150.* 170 Ka'ahumanu Ave., Kahului; (808) 877-0051/(800) 367-5004/(800) 27205275. 148 units, with TV, phones and air-conditioning. Swimming pool, restaurant and cocktail lounge, meeting rooms, shops and beauty salon. Handicapped facilities.

Maui Palms Hotel. *$50-$56.* 150 Ka'ahumanu Ave., Kahului; (808) 877-0071. 103 rooms with TV, phones and air-conditioning. Swimming pool, restaurant and lounge.

Maui Seaside Hotel. *$54-$98.* 100 Ka'ahumanu Ave., Kahului; (808) 877-3311. 192 units; TV, phones, air-conditioning. Swimming pool, restaurant and lounge.

Upcountry

Kula Lodge. *$120-$150.* Haleakala Hwy. (377), Kula; (808) 878-2535/(800) 233-1535. 5 chalet-style units with private lanais, overlooking Central and West Maui. Restaurant and lounge on premises.

Hana

Aloha Cottages. *$55-$75.* Keawa Pl., Hana; (808) 248-8420. 5 rental accommodations, including a studio unit and 3-bedroom house; all units

Historic Pioneer Inn, overlooking Lahaina Harbor

Secluded Makena Beach, on Maui's southwest coast

The Ke'anae Peninsula, covered with taro patches, lies on the road to Hana

Ka'anapali Beach, West Maui

have kitchens, and some have phones.

Hana Bay Vacation Rentals. *$90-$170*. P.O. Box 318, Hana, HI 96713; (808) 248-7727/(800) 959-7727. 14 rental accommodations with TV and phones; some kitchens. Comfortable houses, in various locations in the Hana area.

Hana Kai - Maui Resort. *$110-$125*. Uakea Rd. (near Keanini Dr.), Hana; (808) 248-7482/(800) 346-2772. 20 studio and one-bedroom units; all with kitchens and private lanais. Swimming pool.

Hana Plantation Houses. *$80-$185*. P.O. Box 489, Hana, HI 96713; (808) 248-7248/(800) 657-7723. 12 rental accommodations, ranging from studio units to 2-bedroom cottages; all have TV, phones, and kitchens. Minimum stay: 2 days.

Heavenly-Hana Inn. *$80-$90*. Hana Hwy. (near Uakea Rd.), Hana; (808) 248-8442. 6 self-contained units, including 4 with Japanese decor. TV, kitchenettes, private lanais.

Hotel Hana-Maui. *$305-$525*. Cnr. Hana Hwy. and Keawa Pl., Hana; (808) 248-8211/(800) 321-HANA. 96-room luxury hotel, with in-room phones. Hotel facilities include a swimming pool and spa, tennis court, 3-hole golf course, restaurants and cocktail lounge, meeting rooms, shops and beauty salon.

BED & BREAKFAST INNS

Ahinahina Farm Bed & Breakfast. *$85-$95*. 210 Ahinahina Pl., Kula; (808) 878-6096. Situated in Maui's Upcountry, with views of Mt. Haleakala and Ma'alaea Bay. 2 guest units, including a private studio and a 2-bedroom cottage. Private baths, and kitchens. Continental breakfast. Minimum stay, 3 nights.

Anuhea Bed & Breakfast Health Retreat. *$50-$95*. 3164 Mapu Pl., Kihei; (808) 874-1490/(800) 206-4441. 4 guest rooms, most with private baths; TV, phones; some ocean views. Minimum stay, 3 days.

Bloom Cottage. *$90-$95*. Kula Hwy. (37), Kula; (808) 878-1425. 2-bedroom cottage, situated at an elevation of 3,000 feet, with superb views of West Maui, Lanai and Kahoolawe. Laura Ashley-style furnishings; full kitchen. Complimentary juice and muffins.

Garden Gate Bed & Breakfast. *$50-$95*. 67 Kaniau Rd., Lahaina; (808) 661-8800. Located near beach. Offers 2 guest rooms with TV, phones and air-conditioning. Hearty country breakfast. Minimum stay, 3 days.

Haikuleana Bed & Breakfast. *$80-$90*. 69 Haiku Rd., Haiku; (808) 575-2890. Historic, 1850s plantation home, located one and one-half miles from the beach. Features 4 antique-furnished guest rooms, with private baths. Full breakfast.

Lahaina Hotel. *$89-$129*. 127 Lahainaluna Rd., Lahaina; (808) 661-0577. 13-unit hotel, situated in the center of Lahaina township. Guest rooms feature private lanais. Continental breakfast.

SEASONAL EVENTS

February

First Week. *Maui Marine Art Expo.* Held in the lobby of Stouffer's Wailea Beach Resort, Wailea. Art exhibition featuring works of marine artists from around the world, staged throughout the months of February and March. Free admission. For more information, call (808) 879-4900.

Second Weekend. *Asahi Beer Kyosan Golf Tournament.* Held at the Wailea Blue Course in Wailea. Features professional and celebrity golfers from Japan, both men and women, with a total prize of 20,000,000 yen. For more information, call (808) 879-4465.

Fourth Weekend. *LPGA Women's Kemper Open Golf Tournament.* At the Wailea Blue Course, Wailea. Nationally-televised, prestigious annual tournament, with a prize of $400,000. More information on (808) 879-2966.

March

First Weekend. *Maui Marathon.* 26-mile marathon, beginning at the Maui Mall in Kahului and ending at Whaler's Village, Ka'anapali. More than 300 runners participate. (808) 871-6441.

Third Weekend. *Na Mele O'Maui Festival.* Held at the Ka'anapali Beach Resort. Colorful festival of Hawaiiana; features arts and crafts shows, music, dance, and a children's singing competition. For a schedule, call (808) 661-3271.

April

First Weekend. *Buddha Day.* Celebration of the birth of Buddha, with Buddhist festivities, including flower pageants, staged at Buddhist temples throughout the islands. For more information, call (808) 536-7044. *Marui/O'Neil Invitational.* Held at the Hookipa and Kanaha beaches in Paia. Prestigious windsurfing competition, drawing world-class windsurfers, all vying for a $150,000 prize. 10-day event. (808) 572-4883. *Art Maui.* At the Hui Noeau Visual Arts Center in Makawao. Multi-media event, featuring an exhibition of works of some 300 Maui artists. Exhibitions are staged throughout the month. For more information, call (808) 878-1568.

Second Weekend. *Ritz-Carlton Kapalua Celebration of the Arts.* Held at the Ritz Carlton Hotel, Kapalua. More than 30 local artists offer hands-on lessons in traditional and contemporary Hawaiian art. (808) 669-6200.

May

First Weekend. *Lei Day Celebration.* Celebration of Hawaiian leis, with an island-wide lei-making competition, held at the Maui Inter-Continental Hotel in Wailea. Features colorful leis, made from flowers, feathers and shells; also crowning of Lei Queen and statewide hula competition. (808) 879-1922.

Second Weekend. *Hard Rock Cafe World Cup of Windsurfing.* Held at the Hookipa Beach Park, near Paia. International windsurfing competition, focusing on wave performance. Features top-rated windsurfers from 15 countries, with $50,000 in prize money. For a schedule and more information, call (808) 579-9765.

Third Weekend. *Kapalua Tennis Junior Vet/Senior Championship.* At the Kapalua Tennis Garden, Kapalua. Largest tennis tournament of its kind in the state, with matches scheduled for men and women 35 years and older. More information on (808) 669-5677.

Fourth Weekend. *Barrio Day.* Filipino cultural festival, held at the War Memorial Complex in Wailuku. Features arts and crafts, games, food, and the crowning of Miss Barrio. More information on (808) 877-0220. *Ho'omana'o Challenge.* 75-mile outrigger-canoe race, with 6-man teams, beginning at the Whaler's Village in Ka'anapali and finishing at Waikiki Beach, on the island of Oahu. For more information, call (808) 325-7400.

June

First Weekend. *Kapalua Music Festival.* At the Kapalua Bay Hotel, Kapalua. Features two weekends of chamber music, performed by international and local musicians. For a schedule of performances, call the Maui Philharmonic Society at (808) 669-0244.

Second Weekend. *Kamehameha Day.* Annual celebration honoring Hawaii's first monarch, King Kamehameha I. Festivities held throughout the island; also colorful parade down Front Street in Lahaina. (808) 871-8691. *Maui County Slalom Championships.* Windsurfing competitions held at Kanaha Beach Park. For more information, call (808) 877-2111. *Annual Upcountry Fair.* Old-fashioned farm fair held at the Eddie Tam Center, Makawao. Live entertainment and agricultural exhibits. For schedule, contact Maui Visitors Bureau (808) 244-3530.

July

First Weekend. *4th of July.* Fireworks and Independence Day celebrations held at Wailuku's War Memorial stadium in Wailuku. *Lantern Boat Ceremony/Bon Dance.* Jodo Mission, Lahaina. Buddhist ceremony honoring the souls of the dead. Festivities include a variety of games; also food concessions. For more information, call (808) 661-4304. *Makawao Rodeo.* Largest rodeo in the islands, with more than 300 contestants and $50,000 in prize money. Features 3 days of Western events, including horse races, bareback riding, roping, and country entertainment. Also parade through the town of Makawao. For a schedule of events and more information, call (808) 572-9928. *Wailea Open Tennis Tournament.* Held at the Wailea Tennis Club, Wailea. The event is part of the Grand Prix Tennis Tournament, open to Hawaii residents and USTA members. $10,000 in prizes. (808) 879-1958.

Third Weekend. *Kapalua Wine Symposium.* At the Kapalua Bay Hotel, Kapalua. Wine tasting, and panel discussions with wine and food experts. More information on (808) 669-0244. *Annual Maui Jaycees Carnival.* At the War Memorial Complex in Wailuku. Popular annual carnival, drawing crowds of around 50,000. Carnival rides, games, food, entertainment. More information on (808) 879-0786.

Fourth Weekend. *Maui County Slalom Race Championships.* Kanaha Beach Park, Paia. Windsurfing slalom competitions, featuring windsurfers from around the world. For more information, call (808) 877-2111.

August

First Weekend. *Maui Onion Festival.* Held at the Whaler's Village in Ka'anapali. Three-day celebration of the Maui onion, featuring a variety of food prepared with the famous onions. Also arts and crafts, and entertainment. (808) 661-4567.

Second Weekend. *Hawaii State Slalom Championships.* Windsurfing competition, held at the Kanaha Beach Park in Paia. Features Hawaii's best windsurfers. (808) 877-2111.

Third Weekend. *Annual Haleakala Run to the Sun.* Popular annual event. The 36.2-mile marathon begins at the Maui Mall in Kahului, at sea level, and finishes at the top of Mt. Haleakala, at an elevation of 10,023 feet. (808) 871-6441.

September

First Weekend. *Kapalua Open Tennis Tournament.* Held at the Kapalua Tennis Garden in Kapalua. Largest open tennis tournament in the state, with a prize of $10,000. Features some of Hawaii's top-seeded professional players. More information on (808) 669-0244.

Third Weekend. *Taste of Lahaina.* 30 local restaurants present cooking demonstrations, wine tasting and live entertainment. Free admission; for more information call (808) 667-9175. *Hana Relay.* 54-mile relay race, with 6-person teams, from Kahului to Hana. For more information, call (808) 871-6441.

October

Second Weekend. *Hula O Na Keiki Competition.* At the Ka'anapali Beach Hotel in Ka'anapali. Lively hula festival, with a variety of dance competitions, including individual competitions featuring young Hawaiian hula dancers. For more information, call (808) 661-0011. *Maui County Fair.* Held at the War Memorial Complex, Wailuku. Popular four-day event, drawing more than 90,000 people. Features a traditional fair with carnival rides, food concessions, games and entertainment, and livestock and other exhibits. (808) 244-7643.

Third Weekend. *Maui County Rodeo.* Held at the Oskie Rice Arena in Makawao. Two-day event, drawing real "paniolos" — Hawaiian cowboys — from throughout the island. Variety of Western events, including cow-roping competitions, bucking bulls, horse races, bareback riding and trick riding. For a schedule of events, call (808) 572-9928. *Aloha Week.* Week-long festival, with events staged throughout the island, at the Ka'anapali Beach Resort, Kihei, Wailea, Wailuku and Kahului. Features a variety of Hawaiian pageantry and demonstrations in lei making, poi pounding, coconut husking, coconut weaving and Hawaiian style of quilting. Also parades, arts and crafts, food, island fruit tasting, canoe races, and entertainment — including original Hawaiian music and hula dancers. For a schedule of events and more information, call (808) 944-8857.

Fourth Weekend. *Ka'anapali Classic Senior PGA Tour golf Tournament.* Top PGA senior players compete in 54-hole tournament at Ka'anapali's North Course. Also includes a 2-day Pro-Am tournament. (808) 661-3271. *Aloha Classic.* Held at Hookipa Beach Park, just east of Paia. 10-day event, comprising the Pro Windsurfing World Cup Final. Top windsurfers from 20 different countries compete for the $180,000 prize. More information on (808) 575-9151. *Halloween Parade.* Front Street, Lahaina. Includes a parade, costume contest, and a street party from 4.30 p.m. until midnight on the 31st. More information on (808) 667-9175.

November

Third Week. *Kapalua International Championship of Golf.* Hosted by the Kapalua Golf Club at the Kapalua Bay Resort. Features some of the top-seeded PGA golfers, with a total prize of $880,000. For information, call (808) 669-0244.

Fourth Week. *Maui Invitational.* Pre-season NCAA basketball tournament, held at the Lahaina Civic Center in Lahaina. More information on (808) 661-4685.

December

First Weekend. *Bodhi Day.* Traditional Buddhist celebrations at temples throughout islands, marking the Buddhist Day of Enlightenment. For more information, call (808) 536-7044. *Kapalua Betsy Nagelson Pro-Am Invitational Tennis Tournament.* At the Kapalua Tennis Garden, in Kapalua. Women's doubles tennis tournament, featuring 18 teams, in which professional players team up with amateurs. For a schedule, call (808) 669-5677.

Second Weekend. *Na Mele O Maui Song Contest and Hula Festival.* Two-day festival held at the Hyatt Regency and Maui Marriott in Ka'anapali. Features traditional Hawaiian song contests and a "Best of the Best" hula competition. For more information, call (808) 661-3271.

PLACES OF INTEREST

Lahaina and Ka'anapali

Baldwin Home. Cnr. Front and Dickenson Sts., Lahaina; (808) 661-3262. Former home of missionary-physician Reverend Dwight Baldwin, originally built in 1838, from coral, stone and timber, and now fully restored. The house is now a living museum, filled with original furnishings and several personal and household items of the Baldwin family, including old photographs. Open daily, 9-4.30; admission fee: $3.00.

Master's Reading Room. Cnr. Front and Dickenson Sts., Lahaina. Located adjacent to the Baldwin Home, this is one of the oldest structures in Maui, dating from 1833, and originally used as storage space by early missionaries, and later on as an officers' club for ship captains, masters and officers. Now restored, the Reading Room houses the offices of the Lahaina Restoration Foundation. Open during business hours.

Banyan Tree. Located at the corner of Front and Hotel Sts. in Lahaina. This is one of the oldest and largest trees of its kind in the islands, planted in 1873, by Lahaina Sheriff W.O. Smith, to commemorate the 50th anniversary of the arrival of the missionaries in Lahaina. Covers approximately an acre of land, with branches extending nearly 50 yards, supported by aerial roots, which grow downward into the ground to support the tree.

Old Courthouse. Located on the harbor side of the Banyan Tree Square (near the Banyan Tree), in Lahaina. The old center of government activities, originally built in 1857, including in it a jail. The courthouse and jail now house two art galleries. Open during business hours.

Pioneer Inn. Cnr. Front and Hotel Sts., Lahaina; (808) 661-3636. Historic, 48-room inn, located adjacent to the Banyan Tree, overlooking Lahaina Harbor. The inn was originally built in 1901, and is reflective, in its architecture and decor, of Lahaina's whaling period, with antique whaling equipment and photographs of 19th-century whaling expeditions adorning its walls. Now houses two restaurants, a bar, and shops; also offers overnight accommodations.

Brig *Carthaginian II*. Anchored in the Lahaina Harbor, directly across from Pioneer Inn, in Lahaina; (808) 661-3262. Authentically restored, square-rigged brig; replica of the 19th-century ship that brought the first missionaries to the islands. Now houses a small museum below deck, with exhibits on whales and whaling, and also ongoing film on whaling. Museum hours: 9-4.30 daily. Admission fee: $3.00.

Hale Pa'ahao. Cnr. Prison and Waine'e Sts., Lahaina. Old stone jail (Hale Pa'ahao means "stuck in irons house"), built in 1854, from coral blocks taken from Lahaina's Old Fort at the Banyan Square. The jail has been largely preserved in its original state, much as it appeared in the 1850s, with one cell displaying a mannequin of an old salt, and another a list of convictions handed down in the 1860s and 1870s, as well as a diary of an inmate once confined to the cell. Open daily, 9-5. Free admission.

Wailoa Church. Waine'e St., Lahaina. Formerly the Waine'e Church; originally built in 1823, and destroyed and rebuilt several times over the years, the last in 1988, when it was renamed "Wailoa." The church is significant in that Keopuolani, wife of Kamehameha I and mother of Kamehameha II and Kamehameha III, converted to Christianity here. There is also an ancient cemetery located adjacent to the church, the *Wailoa Cemetery*, where Hawaiian royalty and early missionaries are buried.

Wo Hing Society Temple. Located on Front St., north from the center of town, in Lahaina. Historic Chinese temple, originally built in 1812 as a fraternal and social meeting hall for Hawaii's Chinese population. Now houses a museum, devoted to Chinese culture, with Chinese artifacts and exhibits, including a Taoist shrine. There is also a small, historic theater adjacent to the temple, the *Cookhouse Theatre*, which features some fascinating old films of Hawaii, shot by Thomas Edison in 1898. The theater and museum are open to the public daily 9-4. (808) 661-3262.

Jodo Mission. Located on Ala Moana St. (which is a continuation of Front St.), approximately a mile north of downtown Lahaina. Features one of the largest Buddha statues — cast in bronze — outside Asia, erected in 1968, to commemorate the centennial of the arrival of the first Japanese immigrants in Hawaii, in 1868. The mission park is open to the public.

Hale Pai. Housed in the Lahainaluna Seminary, at the end of Lahainaluna Rd., just outside Lahaina. Hale Pai — meaning "house of printing" — is one of the oldest printing presses in the West, where the first Hawaiian-language newspaper was printed in 1834. It now houses a small museum, with displays of samples of some of the early type and printing, including some first editions of books printed here in the 1830s, and a replica of the original Ramage printing press. Open 10-3.30, Mon.-Fri.; donations accepted. (808) 661-3262/667-7040.

Atlantis Submarine Museum. 505 Front St., Lahaina; (808) 667-6604. Displays of old photographs and drawings and other exhibits depicting the history of underwater technology, from the time of Alexander the Great to present day. Open daily, 8-6; free admission.

Whalers Village Museum. 2435 Ka'anapali Pkwy., Bldg. G-8, Ka'anapali; (808) 661-5992. Houses exhibits and artifacts centered around Maui's whaling era, including old photographs, charts, compasses, bone hooks, guns, spears and other weapons and tools used in whaling. Also displays depicting whale biology, with a description of how the different parts of a whale are used — including whale bone — and how oil is extracted from whale blubber. Open daily, 9.30 a.m.-10 p.m. Free admission.

Central Maui

Alexander & Baldwin Sugar Museum. Cnr. Pu'unene Ave. (Hwy. 350) and Hansen Rd., Pu'unene (south of Kahului); (808) 871-8058. Houses an extensive collection of artifacts depicting the history of Maui's sugar industry, including old photographs of sugar mill and sugarcane field workers, and portraits of members of the Alexander and Baldwin families. Also on display are scale models of the original Alexander & Baldwin sugar mill, and exhibits describing the sugar-making process — from the planting and harvesting of the sugarcane, to the processing and bagging of the sugar. Open 9.30-4.30, Mon.-Sat. Admission fee: $3.00 adults, $1.50 children.

Kanaha Pond State Wildlife Sanctuary. Located off Hana Hwy. (36), near the intersection of Haleakala Hwy. (396), just east of Kahului. Wildlife preserve, where Hawaiian stilts, Hawaiian coots, and other endangered species of such indigenous wildlife can be seen. There is also an observation shelter here, overlooking the pond and marshlands of the sanctuary.

Maui Zoological and Botanical Gardens. Located on Kanaloa Ave., $\frac{1}{4}$ mile north of the intersection of Ka'ahumanu Ave. (directly across from the Wailuku War Memorial), in Wailuku. Comprises a small zoo, with some exotic birds, monkeys, goats and other such animals; and a botanical garden, with a small display of indigenous Hawaiian plants and flowers. Open daily; free admission.

Ka'ahumanu Church. Cnr. Main and High Sts., Wailuku. Picturesque, New England-style church, dating from 1837 and named for Queen Ka'ahumanu, the favorite wife of King Kamehameha I, and one Maui's first converts to Christianity. The church offers Hawaiian services on Sundays.

Hale Hoikeike - Bailey House Museum. 2375-A Main St., Wailuku; (808) 244-3326. Former home of New England missionary Edward Bailey, built between 1833 and 1850. Now houses a museum, devoted to Hawaiian and missionary history. Also features a collection of Reverend Bailey's art, depicting scenes from the early and mid-1800s. Open 10-4.30, Mon.-Fri. Admission fee: $3.00 adults, $1.00 children.

Tropical Gardens of Maui. Located on Iao Valley Rd., $\frac{1}{4}$ mile west of Main St., in Wailuku; (808) 244-3085. Well-kept botanical gardens, featuring several species of native Hawaiian plants, as well as plants introduced to the Hawaiian islands. Open 9-5 daily; admission fee: $4.00 adults, $2.00 children.

Kepaniwai Heritage Gardens. Situated on Iao Valley Rd., approximately 2 miles west of Wailuku, in the Iao Valley. Scenic public park; features examples of art and architecture depicting the ethnic diversity of the island, including a typical Hawaiian grass hut, a Japanese pagoda surrounded by Japanese gardens and sculpture, a Portuguese villa, a New England salt-box, and Chinese, Filipino and Korean dwellings. The park also offers good picnicking possibilities. Open to the public daily.

Iao Valley State Park. Situated at the end of Iao Valley Rd., some 3 miles west of Wailuku. 4-acre park in delightful valley setting. The park has in it, more or less at the center of it, the picturesque Iao Needle, a 1,200-foot, moss-covered stone spire, which has the distinction of being one of the most photographed sights in Maui. The park also has good hiking and picnicking possibilities.

Maui Tropical Plantation. Located on Honoapi'ilani Hwy. (30), 3 miles south of Wailuku. This is one of Maui's foremost tourist attractions, where a tram whisks visitors through groves of mango, guava, papaya, banana and macadamia nut trees, and sections of coffee and Hawaiian flowers, as well as pineapple and sugarcane fields. There is also a restaurant at the plantation, with all-you-can-eat tropical luncheon buffets, and a market featuring fresh, locally-grown produce. Open 8-5 daily; free admission. Tour cost: $8.00 adults/#3.00 children.

Upcountry

Hui Noeau Visual Arts Center. On Baldwin Ave. (Hwy. 390), between mile markers 5 and 6, Makawao; (808) 572-6560. Housed in the Baldwin Memorial Home, formerly the home of plantation owners Henry and Ethel Baldwin, dating from 1917. The arts center features a variety of art shows, workshops, and classes on ceramics, landscape painting and jewelry making. Permanent and changing exhibits. Gift shop on premises. Gallery hours: 10-4, Tues.-Sun.

Kula Botanical Gardens. Kekaulike Rd. (377), Kula; (808) 878-1715. Offers a variety of Hawaiian and exotic plants and flowers — including several types of proteas, orchids and ginger — as well as native kukui and koa trees. Open 9-4 daily; admission: $3.00 adults, 50¢ children.

Maui Enchanting Gardens. Kula Highway (37), Kula; (808) 878-2531. 8-acre botanical garden, featuring lush tropical plants and a variety of native fruit trees. Gift shop on premises. Hours: 9-5 daily. Admission fee: $3.50 adults/$1.50 children.

Polipoli Springs State Recreation Area. Located approximately 5 miles south of Kula, at the end of Waipoli Rd. (which goes off Kekaulike Ave., 377, a half mile north of Kula Hwy., 37). Densely forested park, situated at an elevation of 6,200 feet, on the slopes of Mt. Haleakala. Offers several miles of well-marked hiking trails, winding through groves of pine, cypress, eucalyptus and redwood; also camping possibilities. Open daily.

Protea Farms. There are a handful of protea farms in the Kula area, open to the public for tours and retail sales, offering more than 30 varieties of the flower. The following are among the most prominent: *Cloud's Rest Protea Farm,* 485-F Upper Kimo Dr., Kula, (808) 878-2544; *Hawaii Protea Cooperative,* at the Kula Lodge, Haleakala Hwy. (377), Kula, (808) 878-2525; and *Sunrise Market & Protea Farm,* 416-A Hwy. 378, Kula, (808) 878-1600. For hours of operation and availability of flowers, call the respective farms.

Tedeschi Vineyards. Located on Kula Hwy. (37), 9 miles south of Kula, at Ulupalakua; (808) 878-6058. This is Hawaii's only winery, situated on the slopes of Mt. Haleakala, established in 1973. It offers four different grape wines — including two sparkling wines and a wine produced from the Carnelian grape — and a pineapple wine. Open for wine tasting and sales daily, 9-5; winery tours every half-hour, 9.30 a.m.-2.30 p.m.

Haleakala National Park. Situated 37 miles southeast of Kahului, more or less in the center of the island, and reached by way of Haleakala Hwy. (37) southeast from Kahului to Pukalani (7 miles), then Hwy. 377 directly south another 6 miles, from where Haleakala Crater Rd. (Hwy. 378) goes off eastward, 12 miles, to the park; (808) 572-7749. 27,000-acre park, which has in it the 10,023-foot Mt. Haleakala, the largest dormant volcano in the world, with a crater that is 3,000 feet deep, $7\frac{1}{2}$ miles long and $2\frac{1}{2}$ miles wide. Offers good hiking possibilities, including a trail that loops through the crater; also picnicking, camping and horseback riding. There is also a Visitors Center at the park, with exhibits and information on the geology and eruption history of Haleakala. Admission fee: $4.00 per car, buses and hikers $2.00 per person.

Road to Hana

Twin Falls. Off Hana Hwy. (360), 12 miles east of Paia. A dirt trail goes off the highway just past mile marker 2 (before crossing the highway bridge), journeying inland a little way, following alongside a stream, to two successive waterfalls — the Twin Falls. The two waterfalls are located approximately a mile from the trailhead, off the highway, a quarter mile or so apart. There is also a natural pool at the foot of each of the falls, ideal for swimming.

Ke'anae Arboretum. On Hana Hwy. (360), $\frac{1}{2}$ mile past mile marker 16 (approximately 18 miles northwest of Hana). Features a variety of indigenous Hawaiian plants and trees, including native forest trees, tropical trees introduced to Hawaii, and cultivated Hawaiian plants. Also view irrigated taro patches, and an authentic representation of a Hawaiian rain forest. Self-guided trails. Open daily; free admission.

Kahanu Gardens. Located on Ulaino Rd., which goes off Hana Hwy. (360), approximately 3 miles north of Hana. Delightful, 126-acre tropical botanical garden, now part of the National Tropical Botanical Garden. The garden grows and displays a collection of ethnobotanical plants, and also has in it one of Hawaii's largest *heiaus*, the Pi'ilanihale Heiau, some 50 feet high, and dating from 1270 A.D. There is also a visitor center at the garden, offering guidebooks for self-guided walking tours of the garden. Open 10 a.m.-2 p.m., Tues.-Sat. Admission fee: $5.00 adults, children free.

Helani Gardens. Hana Hwy. (360), Hana; (808) 248-8274. 70-acre drive-through botanical garden, filled with lavish displays of Hawaiian plants, flowers and fruit trees. Open 10-4 daily; admission: $2.00 per person.

Hana Cultural Center. Uakea Rd. (near Keawa Place), Hana; (808) 248-8622. Small, informative museum, displaying various Hawaiian artifacts, including quilts, bowls, and historic photographs. Also visit the adjacent old courthouse and jail cells. Open daily, 10-4. Suggested donation: $2.00.

Fagan Memorial. Located on Lyon's Hill, across from the Hotel Hana Maui (which is situated on the Hana Hwy.), in Hana. A paved walkway leads from the hotel, crossing over the highway, to the memorial atop the hill, comprising a large lava-stone cross, dedicated to Paul Fagan, founder of the Hana Ranch, who died in 1959. There are also good views from the top of the hill, of the ocean and Hana Bay, and the Hana township below.

Hasegawa Store. 5165 Hana Hwy., Hana. Historic, family-run store, piled high with almost every imaginable item — from groceries to lawnmowers to stereo systems. The store is in fact one of the town's leading attractions, immortalized in song and visited by a host of celebrities, including Kris Kristofferson, George Harrison, Burt Reynolds, Carol Burnett, and others. Open during business hours.

Wailua Falls. Located along Hana Hwy. (360), 7 miles south of Hana. Picturesque, 95-foot waterfalls, alongside the highway, offering good photographing opportunities.

Oheo Gulch (Seven Sacred Pools). Pi'ilani Hwy. (31), approximately 10 miles south of Hana. Features more than 20 natural pools, strung along the Oheo Stream. Also offers some good hiking possibilities, with one or two trails leading past waterfalls and through bamboo forests. Views of island of

Hawaii, roughly 30 miles to the south. There is, in addition, a ranger station in the gulch, with useful information on the area.

Palapala Ho'omau Church. Off Pi'ilani Hwy. (31), 12 miles southwest of Hana, in Kipahulu. Historic church, built in 1857, and situated on a bluff overlooking the ocean. There is also a small, seaside cemetery adjacent to the church, which has in it the grave of pioneer aviator Charles A. Lindbergh, and the grassy *Kipahulu Point Park*, with good views of the ocean as well as picnicking possibilities.

BEACHES

Maui has some of the loveliest beaches in the Pacific, sandy, sunny, and in delightful settings. All beaches are public beaches; however, nude bathing at Hawaii's public beaches is prohibited under state law — although some of the beaches continue to be frequented by nudists. Also, a word of caution: several of the beaches on the island are subject to strong under-currents or rip tides, especially in the winter and spring months, making swimming at these beaches, at such times, inadvisable, frequently dangerous; due caution must therefore be exercised at all times when approaching the ocean.

West Maui

Papalaua State Wayside Beach. Located 4½ miles west of Ma'alaea (approximately 10 miles southeast of Lahaina), off Honoapi'ilani Hwy. (30), between mile markers 11 and 12. Roadside beach, bordered by *kiawe* trees. Offers views of the island of Kaho'olawe. Also picnicking, swimming, snorkeling, and surfing.

Ukumehame Beach Park. Half mile west of Papalaua Beach (see above), off Honoapi'ilani Hwy. (30), at mile marker 12. Rocky beach, with large grassy area, ideal for picnicking. Some fishing possibilities.

Punahoa Beach. Off Honoapi'ilani Hwy. (30), at mile marker 14, approximately 7 miles southeast of Lahaina. Popular white-sand beach, with excellent snorkeling possibilities. Also safe swimming conditions in summer. The beach is bordered by *kiawe* trees.

Awalua Beach. Off Hwy. 30, at mile marker 16, 5 miles south of Lahaina. Narrow roadside beach. Good swimming possibilities; sandy bottom. Also some surfing.

Launiupoko State Wayside Beach Park. Located 2½ miles south of Lahaina, off Hwy. 30, near mile marker 18. Rocky beach, with a wading pool for children. Offers views of Kaho'olawe, Lanai and Molokai. Beach facilities include picnic tables, barbecue grills, showers and restrooms, and parking area.

Puamana Beach Park. Located just south of Lahaina, off Hwy. 30. Narrow, sandy beach, with picnic tables and parking facilities. Offers good swimming in summer, and promising surfing conditions just north of the beach.

Wahikuli State Wayside Park. 2 miles north of Lahaina, along Hwy. 30. Popular roadside beach park, with small sandy area and rocky shoreline. Facilities include picnic tables, showers and restrooms. Some swimming and snorkeling possibilities.

Hanakao'o Beach Park. Situated half-mile north of Wahikuli State Wayside Park (approximately $2\frac{1}{2}$ miles north of Lahaina), off Hwy. 30. Offers picnic tables, showers and restroom facilities; also safe swimming conditions. The beach, in fact, borders Ka'anapali Beach to the north, and is a good place to park and stroll along the latter.

Ka'anapali Beach. 4 miles north of Lahaina, at the Ka'anapali Beach Resort, off Honopi'ilani Hwy. (30). This is one of Hawaii's most popular beaches, 3 miles long, fronting on the Ka'anapali resorts, extending from the Hyatt Regency to the Sheraton and north. Offers safe swimming in summer, and some of the best snorkeling on the island, near Black Rock, at the north end of the beach. The beach can be accessed by way of any of several different public access roads; however, parking is limited.

Honokowai Beach Park. Located a mile north of Ka'anapali Beach Resort, off Lower Honoapi'ilani Rd., in Honokowai. Rocky beach, with a large, grassy area with picnic tables. Also showers and restrooms, and parking facilities. Some snorkeling and swimming.

Kahana Beach. 2 miles north of Honokowai Beach (3 miles north of Ka'anapali), off Lower Honoapi'ilani Rd., Kahana. Features a protective reef just offshore, with safe swimming conditions. Also views of Molokai and Lanai. No beach facilities.

Napili Bay. Situated 5 miles north of Ka'anapali, and reached by way of Lower Honoapi'ilani Rd., then either Hui Drive or Napili Place, with public access roads leading down from these to the beach. The beach is a lovely, white-sand, crescent-shaped beach, bordered by condominium resorts, and offering excellent swimming and snorkeling possibilities in calm seas.

Kapalua Beach. Situated at Kapalua, bordering Kapalua Bay Hotel, with a public access just past Napili Kai Beach Club, off Lower Honoapi'ilani Rd. Beautiful, white-sand cove, with superb views of the island of Molokai. Offers good diving and snorkeling possibilities, and safe swimming. Beach facilities include restrooms and showers; limited parking.

D.T. Fleming Beach Park. Off Hwy.30, at mile marker 31, approximately a mile east of Kapalua. Long, sandy beach, bordered by ironwood trees and shallow sand dunes. Offers picnic tables, barbecue grills, showers and restrooms, and phone. Some surfing possibilities; unsafe for swimming, due to dangerous under-currents.

Mokuleia Beach (Slaughterhouse Beach). Situated at the head of Mokuleia Bay, approximately a mile northeast of the D.T. Fleming Beach, just past mile marker 32 on Hwy. 30, with a handful of trails leading from the highway down to the beach. The beach is in fact part of the Honolua-Mokuleia Bay Marine Life Conservation District, quite popular, in summer, with snorkeling and boardsurfing enthusiasts. In winter, however, the strong under-currents make the ocean here rather dangerous. No facilities.

Honolua Bay. Off Honoapi'ilani Hwy. (30), a half-mile past mile marker 33, adjoining to the east of Mokuleia Bay (see above), and reached by way of dirt road from the highway, passing through pineapple fields. This is one of the most popular surfing spots on the island, featured on covers of surfing magazines. Good place to watch world-class surfers, especially in the winter months.

Southwest Coast

Ma'alaea Beach. Situated just north of Kihei, off N. Kihei Rd. (Hwy. 31). Three-mile-long beach, with strong afternoon winds. Beachcombing and jogging possibilities; also some surfing in summer. Swimming and windsurfing not advisable, due to the adverse ocean and wind conditions. No facilities.

Maipoina Oe Iau. Located off S. Kihei Rd., a half-mile south of the intersection of Hwy. 350, in Kihei. Popular windsurfing spot; also offers safe swimming conditions in the summer months. Whale watching in winter and spring. Facilities include restrooms and picnic tables.

Kalepolepo Beach Park. Located just south of mile marker 1 on S. Kihei Rd., Kihei. Small, sandy beach, with safe swimming for children. Also showers and restroom facilities, and parking area.

Kalama Beach Park. Off S. Kihei Rd., $\frac{1}{2}$ mile south of mile marker 3, Kihei. Shoreline park, with picnic tables, restrooms, basketball and tennis courts, soccer field, and baseball diamond. Also parking facilities.

Kamaole Beach Parks (I, II and III). Located off S. Kihei Rd., just past mile marker 4, south of Kihei. Three consecutive beaches, separated only by rocky outcroppings. All three beaches offer safe swimming and good sunbathing possibilities. Kamaole I, in addition, offers bodysurfing possibilities, and Kamaole III features a children's playground. The beaches also have showers and restroom facilities.

Keawakapu Beach. Situated less than a mile south of Kamaole Beach III (approximately 5 miles south of Kihei), and reached by way of one of two access roads — from the intersection of S. Kihei Rd. and Kilohana Dr., or from the end of S. Kihei Rd., $\frac{1}{4}$ mile past mile marker 6. The beach has a sandy bottom, and offers good swimming, bodyboarding and snorkeling possibilities. No facilities.

Mokapu Beach. Situated at Stouffer's Wailea Beach Resort at Wailea; reached by way of a public access road, just to the south of Stouffer's, off Wailea Alanui. Small cove, with a sandy bottom, ideal for swimming and bodysurfing. Also promising snorkeling on calm days. No public facilities.

Ulua Beach. Located just south of Stouffer's Wailea Beach Resort, off Wailea Alanui, at Wailea. Offers good swimming and bodysurfing possibilities, and snorkeling in calm seas. Showers, restrooms, parking area.

Wailea Beach. At the Grand Hyatt and Four Seasons resort hotels in Wailea, with a public access off Wailea Alanui, passing between the two resorts and leading to the beach. The Wailea Beach is a beautiful, white-sand beach, with good swimming, snorkeling and bodysurfing possibilities. Beach facilities include showers and restrooms; also parking area.

Polo Beach. Off Kaukahi Rd. (which goes off Wailea Alanui, just past the Kea Lani Hotel), Wailea. Offers good swimming, snorkeling and bodysurfing; also superb views of Kaho'olawe and Molokini. Showers, restrooms and parking facilities.

Palauea Beach. Located $\frac{1}{4}$ mile south of Polo Beach, off Wailea Alanui; reached by way of a public access road along the shoreline from Polo Beach. Lovely, secluded, sandy beach, bordered by *kiawe* trees. Offers some swimming and bodysurfing possibilities. No beach facilities.

Po'olenalena Beach Park (Paipu Beach). Situated 2 miles south of Wailea, off Makena Alanui. Undeveloped sandy beach, backed by low sand dunes and *kiawe* trees. Good swimming possibilities, except during high surf or kona storms. No facilities.

Makena Landing Beach Park. Just to the south of Po'olenalena Beach (see above), Off Makena Rd., approximately $\frac{1}{2}$ mile from the end of Makena Alanui, at Makena. Small, rocky beach, which is also a popular starting point for scuba diving expeditions. Beach facilities include showers, restrooms and a parking area.

Maluaka Beach Park. At the Maui Prince Hotel, $\frac{1}{2}$ mile south of Makena Landing, accessed from Makena Rd. (which is a continuation of Makena Alanui), in Makena. The beach is wide, crescent-shaped, and backed by shallow, grassy sand dunes and groves of *kiawe* trees. It offers safe swimming conditions, and showers and restroom facilities. Also parking area.

Oneuli Beach (Black Sand Beach). Located on the north side of Pu'u Ola'i (Red Hill); accessed by way of a dirt road that goes off Makena Rd. (continuation of Makena Alanui), approximately 3 miles south of the intersection of Kaukahi Rd. and Makena Alanui. The beach is fronted by a coral reef, making it unsafe for swimming. No beach facilities.

Oneloa Beach (Makena Beach). Situated off Makena Rd., 3 miles south of the intersection of Kaukahi Rd. and Makena Alanui; reached by way of a dirt road that goes off Makena Rd., approximately ¼ mile, toward the ocean. Long, white-sand beach, in idyllic setting; one of the southwest coast's loveliest beaches. Offers good bodysurfing possibilities; also snorkeling along the north end of the beach, just around Red Hill. Swimming, however, is not encouraged due to unpredictable ocean conditions. No facilities. The beach, by the way, is also known as Big Beach.

Puuolai Beach (Little Beach). Off Makena Rd., roughly 3 miles south of the intersection of Kaukahi Rd.; accessed from the north end of Oneloa Beach (see above), over a rocky outcropping. The beach itself is small, sandy, and one of the most popular nudist beaches on Maui. It offers safe swimming conditions, as well as some good bodysurfing possibilities.

Ahihi-Kinau Natural Area Reserve. Located a mile south of Oneloa Beach (approximately 4 miles south of Makena), off Makena Rd. Offers excellent scuba diving and snorkeling possibilities. Fishing, hunting and removal of coral and lava prohibited. Unsafe ocean conditions during high surf. No facilities.

La Perouse Bay. Situated 1½ miles south of Ahihi-Kinau Natural Area Reserve, at the end of Makena Rd. Undeveloped beach area. Offers good scuba diving and snorkeling possibilities, but is generally unsafe for swimming. Ruins of ancient fishing village nearby, on the inland side of the historic Hoapili Trail which heads out eastward.

Central Maui

Waihe'e Beach Park. Situated near the Waiehu Municipal Golf Course, off Halewaiu Rd. (which goes off Kahekili Hwy., 340), in Waihe'e. Narrow, gray-sand beach, frequented primarily by fishermen. Some beachcombing possibilities. Also picnic tables, showers, restrooms, and parking facilities.

Waiehu Beach Park. Located at the end of Lower Waiehu Beach Rd., which goes off Kahekili Hwy. (340), in Waiehu. Narrow, sandy beach, frequented primarily by fishermen. Beachcombing. No facilities.

Kanaha Beach Park. Situated off Alahao St., near the Kahului Airport, in Kahului. Popular sandy beach, bordered by kiawe trees. Offers safe swimming for children, and good windsurfing and surfing possibilities. Picnic tables, barbecue grills, showers and restrooms.

H.A. Baldwin Park. Located just west of Paia, off Hana Hwy. (36), at mile marker 6. Well-liked beach, especially popular with swimmers, bodysurfers and picnickers. Offers picnic tables, showers and restrooms, a pavilion, and a baseball and soccer field.

Hookipa Beach Park. Off Hana Hwy. (36), 2 miles east of Paia. This is one of the most popular windsurfing and surfing spots on the island, and the site of several national and international windsurfing competitions. Not suitable for swimming.

Hana

Pa'iloa Beach. At the Waianapanapa State Park (2 miles north of Hana), off Hana Hwy., at mile marker 32. Small, black-sand beach, with picnic area. Swimming not advised due to prevailing strong ocean currents.

Hana Beach Park. Situated along the southeast end of Hana Bay, and reached on Keawa Place, which goes off the Hana Hwy. (360). Popular local beach; offers one of safest swimming areas on East Maui. Also good snorkeling possibilities, in the section between the beach pier and lighthouse. Picnic tables, showers, and restrooms.

Kaihalulu Beach (Red Sand Beach). Off Wakea Rd., Hana; reached by way of a trail leading from the south end of Wakea Rd. down to the beach. Small beach area, comprising largely a volcanic cinder. Unsafe for swimming.

Koki Beach Park. Situated approximately $1\frac{1}{2}$ miles southeast of Hana, off Haneoo Rd., which goes off Pi'ilani Hwy. (31). Popular surfing and bodysurfing beach, bordered by ironwood trees. Picnic tables, barbecue pits. Unsafe for swimming.

Hamoa Beach Park. Located at the head of Mokae Cove, off Haneoo Rd. (which goes off Hwy. 31), $2\frac{1}{2}$ miles south of Hana. The beach is used almost exclusively by guests of the Hotel Hana Maui. Offers good surfing and bodysurfing possibilities; also safe swimming in calm weather. No public access.

GOLF COURSES

Kapalua Golf Club. At the Kapalua Bay Resort, Kapalua; (808) 669-8044. The golf club has three notable courses — *The Plantation at Kapalua*, a newly-built, 18-hole, Ben Crenshaw-designed, situated on 250 acres, par 72 and 7,100 yards; and the 18-hole, Arnold Palmer-designed *Kapalua Village* and *Kapalua Bay* courses, both 72 par. Pro shop, driving range, club rentals, and restaurant on premises. Green fees (at all 3 courses): $120.00 (including cart), and $60.00 during twilight hours.

Makena Golf Course. 5415 Makena Alanui, Makena; (808) 879-3344. 18-hole, championship course, designed by Robert Trent Jones, Jr.; 6,739 yards, par 72. Green fees: $120.00 (including cart), $60.00 during twilight hours. Pro shop, driving range, and club rentals; also restaurant on premises.

Pukalani Country Club. 360 Pukalani, Pukalani; (808) 572-1314. 18-hole course; 6,570 yards, par 72. Green fees: $65.00 (including cart). Pro shop, driving range, club rentals, and restaurant.

Royal Ka'anapali Golf Courses. Located at the Ka'anapali Beach Resort, off Hwy.30; (808) 661-3691. Offers two 18-hole, par-72 courses; the *North Course* is designed by Robert Trent Jones, Jr., and the *South Course* by Jack Snyder. Green fees (for both courses): $100.00 (including cart), $60.00 twilight hours. Pro shop, driving range, club rentals, and restaurant

Sandalwood Golf Course. 2500 Honoapi'ilani Hwy. (30), Waikapu; (808) 242-7090. Newly-built 18-hole course; 6,500 yards, par 72. Green fees: $75.00 (including cart). Facilities include a pro shop, driving range, and club rentals. Also restaurant on premises.

Silversword Golf Club. 1345 Pi'ilani Hwy., Kihei; (808) 874-0777. 18-hole course; par 71, 6,801 yards. Green fees: $65.00 (including cart),

$45.00 twilight hours. Pro shop, driving range, club rentals, restaurant.

Waiehu Municipal Golf Course. Off Kahekili Hwy. (340), Waiehu (2 miles north of Wailuku); (808) 243-7400. Oceanfront course; 18 holes, par 72. Green fees: $30.00. Pro shop, driving range, and restaurant. Cart and club rentals.

Wailea Golf Courses. Wailea Alanui, Wailea; (808) 879-2966. There are three 18-hole, par-72, Jack Snyder-designed golf courses here — the challenging *Blue Course*, which features 42 lakes and 72 bunkers; the *Orange Course*, with its abundant trees and lava rock; and the newly-built 7,000-yard *Gold Course*. Green fees (for all 3 courses): $125.00 (including cart). Pro shop, and club rentals. Restaurant on premises.

TENNIS

Hyatt Regency Maui. 200 Nohea Kai Dr., Ka'anapali; (808) 661-1234, ext. 3174. Offers 5 hard courts. Pro shop, lessons.

Kapalua Tennis Garden. 100 Kapalua Dr., Kapalua; (808) 669-5677. 10 courts, including 4 lighted courts for night play. Pro shop, lessons, rentals. Court fee: $10.00 per day.

Makena Tennis Club. At the Maui Prince Hotel, 5400 Makena Alanui, Makena; (808) 879-8777. 6 courts. Lessons, rentals. Court fee: $10.00 per day, $5.00 for hotel guests.

Maui Marriott Resort. 100 Nohea Kai Dr., Ka'anapali; (808) 667-1200. 5 courts, including 3 with lights. Pro shop, lessons, rentals. Court fee: $7.50 an hour, $6.00 for hotel guests.

Royal Lahaina Tennis Ranch. 2780 Kekaa Dr., Ka'anapali; (808) 661-3611, ext. 2296. 11 courts, including 6 lighted courts; also stadium court. Pro shop, lessons, rentals. Court fee: $10.00 per day, $6.00 for hotel guests.

Sheraton Maui. 2605 Ka'anapali Pkwy., Ka'anapali; (808) 661-0031, ext. 5197. Offers 3 courts with lights. Pro shop, lessons, rentals. Court fee: $12.00 per hour.

Wailea Tennis Club. 131 Wailea Ike Place, Wailea; (808) 879-1958. Offers 11 championship hard courts, including 3 lighted courts for night play. Also 3 superb grass courts. Pro shop, rentals. Grass court fee: $25.00 per day, $20.00 for resort guests; hard court fee: $15.00 per day, $10.00 for hotel guests.

Public Tennis Courts. *Lahaina Civic Center,* Hwy. 30 (across from Wahikuli State Wayside Park), Lahaina; 2 courts with lights. *Malu-ulu-olele Park,* cnr. Front and Shaw Sts., Lahaina; 4 courts, with lights. *Kalama Park,* S. Kihei Rd. (½ mile south of mile marker 3), Kihei; 2 courts with lights. *Maui Community College,* cnr. Ka'ahumanu Ave. and Wakea Rd., Wailuku; 4 courts. *Wailuku War Memorial,* Ka'ahumanu Ave. (Hwy. 32), at mile marker 1, Wailuku; 4 lighted courts. *Hana Ball Park,* cnr. Hauoli St. and Uakea Rd., Hana; 2 courts with lights. *Eddie Tam Memorial Center,* Hwy. 377 (½ mile west of the intersection of Baldwin Ave.), Makawao; 2 courts, with lights. *Pukalani Community Center,* Pukalani St. (which goes off Haleakala Hwy., 37, midway between mile markers 6 and 7), Pukalani; 2 courts with lights.

TOURS

Helicopter Tours

Helicopter tours are quite popular on Maui, and a good way to see the island, with several different companies offering flights over West Maui, the Haleakala crater, the Hana area and other parts of the island. Tours originate at the Kahului Heliport in Kahului, and tour companies, typically, utilize any of three different types of helicopters — the Aero-Star, a 6-seater, with all seats by the windows, offering good views to all passengers; the Hughes 500, a 4-seater, which also offers window seating to all passengers; and the Bell Jet Ranger, another 4-seater, which, nevertheless, has only three window seats, with one passenger being confined to a center seat and, consequently, lesser views. Tours last anywhere from 45 minutes to 1 hour and 45 minutes, and cost $99-$200 per person.

Helicopter Tour Companies. *Alexair,* (808) 871-0792/(800) 462-2281; *Blue Hawaiian Helicopters,* (808) 871-8844/(800) 247-5444; *Cardinal Helicopters,* (808) 877-2400; *Diamond Helicopters,* (808) 877-3344; *Hawaii Helicopters,* (808) 877-3900/(800) 346-2403; *Helicopter Tours,* (800) 624-7771; *Kenai Helicopters,* (808) 871-6463/(800) 622-3144; *Papillon Helicopters,* (808) 669-4884/(800) 367-7095; *Sunshine Helicopter Tours,* (808) 871-0722/(800) 544-2520.

Sightseeing Tours

Akina Tours. P.O. Box 933, Kihei, HI 96753; (808) 879-2828. Offers guided tours of Maui's Upcountry and the Haleakala crater, as well as the Road to Hana. Cost of tours ranges from $45-$84.

Grayline - Maui. 273 Dairy Rd., Kahului; (800) 367-2420/(808) 877-5507. Variety of tours, of Lahaina, the Iao Needle State Park, Hana, and the Haleakala crater. Cost of tours ranges from $20-$70.

Heavenly Hana Tours. 148 Shaw St., Lahaina; (808) 661-9955. Offers commuter flights into Hana, and 4½-hour tours of all the points of interest in and around the town; also includes a continental breakfast. Cost of tour: $169.00 per person.

Lahaina-Ka'anapali & Pacific Railroad (Sugarcane Train). Cnr. Lahainaluna Rd. and Hinau Rd., Lahaina; and cnr. Honoapi'ilani Hwy. (30) and Puukolii Rd., Ka'anapali; (808) 661-0089. Historic, 19th-century steam train. Operates between Lahaina and Ka'anapali, daily from 9.30 a.m. until 5.30 p.m., passing by sugarcane fields. Trains depart from each end — from the Lahaina and Ka'anapali stations — every 40 minutes; train rides are approximately 1 hour each way. Fare: $12.00 adults, $6.00 children (one-way).

Local Guides of Maui. First Insurance Plaza, Kahului; (808) 877-4042/(800) 228-6284. Personal guides escort you in your car, pinpointing all the places of local interest on the island; 8-hour tours. Cost: $165.00.

Polynesian Adventure Tours. 431 Alamaha St., Kahului; (808) 877-4242. Day tours of Haleakala and the Iao Valley; also Road to Hana. Cost of tours: $42-$69 per person.

Robert's Hawaii. Kaonawai Pl., Kahului; (808) 973-2300. Offers narrated tours of Haleakala, Hana and the Iao Valley. Cost of tours: $18-$48 per person.

Temptation Tours. RR 1, P.O. Box 454, Kula, HI 96790; (808) 877-8888. Custom tours of Hana, combining helicopter rides, and including lunch; originates in Kahului. Cost of tours ranges from $99-$179.

Trans Hawaiian Maui. 845 Palapala Dr., Kahului; (808) 735-6467. Half-day and full-day tours of Lahaina, Hana, the Iao Needle State Park and the Haleakala crater. Cost of tours: half-day tours, $42.00; full-day tours, $70.00.

Hiking Tours

Hawaiian Bicycle Experience. P.O. Box 1874, Kihei, HI 96753; (808) 874-1929. Guided hiking trips to pristine waterfalls and black-sand beaches; also hiking in Maui's Upcountry. 6-hour hikes. Cost: $50.00 per person.

Bicycle Tours

Chris' Bike Adventures. Lower Kula Rd., Kula; (808) 877-8000. Offers coastal and Upcountry tours; also tours of the nearby islands of Molokai and Lanai. Tour cost: Upcountry and Coast tours, $79-$99; Molokai and Lanai tours, $135.00.

Cruiser Bob's Downhill. 99 Hana Hwy., Paia; (808) 667-7717/1579-8444. Daily sunrise and sunset trips, down the slopes of Mt. Haleakala; includes pick-up service and continental breakfast in the morning. Cost: $99.00 per person.

Hawaiian Bicycle Experience. P.O. Box 1874, Kihei, HI 96753; (808) 874-1929. Offers organized bicycle tours throughout Maui, for beginners as well as intermediate and advanced level cyclists. Cost: $50.00 per person.

Maui Downhill Bicycle Tours. 199 Dairy Rd., Kahului; (808) 871-2155. Morning and afternoon rides down Haleakala; includes continental breakfast and pick-up service. Tour cost: $99.00 per person.

Maui Mountain Cruiser's. 353 Hanamau St., Kahului; (808) 871-6014/572-0195. Sunrise and midday rides, down the slopes of Haleakala; includes a continental breakfast. Tour cost: sunrise ride, $99.00; midday ride, $88.00.

Bicycle and Moped Rentals. *A & B Moped Rental,* Napili; (808) 669-0027. *Fun Bike Rentals,* 193 Lahainaluna Rd., Lahaina; (808) 661-3053. *Go Go Bikes,* Lahaina; (808) 661-3063. *Island Sports Rental Connection,* Lahaina; (808) 667-0449. *Kukui Activity Center,* 1819 S. Kihei Rd., Bldg. E, Kihei; (808) 875-1151. *Maui Mac Dougal's,* 1913-C S. Kihei Rd., Kihei; (808) 874-0068. *Paradise Pedaling,* 2439 S. Kihei Rd., Space 101-A, Kihei; (808) 874-5303. *The Island Biker,* Kahului Shopping Center, Kahului; (808) 877-7744. *West Maui Sports,* Lahaina; (808) 667-9393.

Horseback Riding

Adventures on Horseback. Makawao; (808) 242-7445. Five-hour guided rides along the lower slopes of Haleakala, journeying through rain forests; includes breakfast and lunch. Tour cost: $140.00 per person.

Hana Ranch. Hana; (808) 248-8211. Horseback rides along the Hana coast; some of the rides include barbecues and luaus. Cost: $27.50-$100 per person.

Makena Stables. 7299 Makena Rd., Makena; (808) 879-0244. Offers 2½-hour and 3½-hour sunset rides. Cost: 2½-hour rides, $75.00; 3½-hour rides, $95.00.

Pony Express. Haleakala Crater Rd., Kula; (808) 667-2000. Guided, half-day ride through the Haleakala Crater. Also ranch rides in Maui's Upcountry. Tour cost: Haleakala Crater ride, $100.00; Upcountry rides, $30-$50.

Rainbow Ranch. Napili; (808) 669-4991. Offers a variety of rides, to suit all levels of riders; rides are conducted primarily in the West Maui area. Cost: $31-$83 per person.

Sea Horse Ranch. Wailuku; (808) 244-9862. Three-hour trail rides. Cost: $79.00 per person.

Silver Cloud Upcountry Ranch. Thompson Rd., Kula; (808) 878-6101. Scenic rides through Maui's Upcountry; also 2-hour sunset rides. Cost: $40.00 per person.

Thompson Ranch. RR 2, P.O. Box 203, Kula, HI 96790; (808) 878-1910. 1½- to 2-hour horseback rides along the slopes of Haleakala; also full-day trips through the Haleakala Crater, with lunch included. Cost: 1½-hour ride, $35.00; 2-hour ride, $40.00; full-day crater ride, $150.00.

WATER SPORTS

Boat Tours and Snorkeling Excursions

Atlantis Submarines. 505 Front St., Suite 234, Lahaina; (808) 667-2224/(800) 548-6262. Unique submarine excursions aboard a 65-foot submarine, exploring more than 100 feet below the ocean surface, just offshore from Lahaina. One-hour excursions. Tour cost: $65-$90.

Blue Water Rafting. Kihei; (808) 879-RAFT. Variety of snorkeling excursions, including trips to Molokini and Maui's south shore. Cost $39-$75 per person.

Captain Nemo's. 150 Dickenson St., Lahaina; (808) 661-5555. Snorkeling excursions to Lanai; also sunset sails. Cost: Lanai snorkeling excursion, $69.00-$95.00; sunset sail, $32.00.

Captain Zodiac. Front St., Lahaina; (808) 667-5862. Offers half-day and full-day snorkeling excursions to Lanai; also 2½-hour and 3½-hour whale-watching tours, with the latter including some snorkeling. Tour cost: snorkeling excursion, $53-$98; whale-watching tour, $45-$53.

Lin Wa Cruises. Front St., Lahaina; (808) 661-3392. Cruises on board the glass-bottomed *Golden Dragon*, exploring West Maui's coral reefs. 1½-hour cruises; includes soft drinks and fruit juices. Cost: $17.50 adults, and $8.75 children.

Island Marine Activities. 505 Front St., Lahaina; (808) 661-8397. Whale-watching tours; 2½ hours. Cost: $30.00 per person.

Maui Classic Charters. 101 N. Kihei Rd., Suite 7, Kihei; (808) 879-8188/(800) 736-5740. Morning snorkeling expeditions to Molikini, including continental breakfast and a barbecue lunch; also sunset sails with complimentary pupus and entertainment, and whale-watching excursions, including some snorkeling. Cost: snorkeling expedition, $66.00; sunset sail, $64.00; whale-watching tour, $39.00.

Molokini Adventure. Ma'alaea Harbor; (808) 242-7683. Snorkeling excursions to Molokini, including a continental breakfast and deli-style lunch. Tour cost: $49.00 per person.

Ocean Activities Center. 1325 S. Kihei Rd., Suite 212, Kihei; (808) 879-4485/(800) 367-8047, ext. 448. Offers a variety of snorkeling excursions to Molokai and Lanai, including a continental breakfast and deli lunch; also dinner cruises, featuring a prime rib buffet, open bar and entertainment. Cost: snorkeling excursion, $40-$60; dinner cruise, $45-$60.

Ocean Riders. P.O. Box 967, Lahaina, HI 96767; (808) 661-3586/(800) 733-3586. Full-day snorkeling trips to Lanai; includes continental breakfast and lunch. Tour cost: $130.00 adults, $80.00 children. Whale-watching tours $50.00 adults/$35.00 children.

Pacific Whale Foundation. 101 N. Kihei Rd., Kihei; (808) 879-8811. Half-day snorkeling excursions to Molokini; also whale-watching tours. Cost: snorkeling excursion, $54.00; whale-watching tour, $30.00 adults/ $15.00 children; nature cruise $10.00 adults/$5.00 children.

Prince Kuhio. Ma'alaea Harbor; (808) 242-8777. Half-day snorkeling trip to Molokini, including continental breakfast and a luncheon buffet; and dinner cruises. Tour cost: snorkeling trip, $75.00 adults and $40.00 children; dinner cruise, $60.00.

Sail Hawaii. P.O. Box 573, Kihei; (808) 879-2201. Whale-watching and snorkeling excursions, including continental breakfast and deli lunch; and 2-hour sunset sails. Tour cost: whale-watching and snorkeling excursion, $59.00; sunset sail, $40.00-$50.00.

Scotch Mist. Lahaina; (808) 661-0386. Snorkeling and sailing excursions to Lanai and along the coast of West Maui; also whale-watching tours, and sunset sails with complimentary beer, wine, fruit juice and champagne. Cost: snorkeling and sailing excursion, $40-$50; whale-watching tours and sunset sails, $30.00.

Trilogy Excursions. 180 Lahainaluna Rd., Lahaina; (808) 661-4743/(800) 874-2666. Half-day snorkeling expedition to Molokini, including continental breakfast and deli lunch; and day trips to Lanai, with snorkeling and a tour of the island. Also 2-hour whale-watching tours. Cost of tours: full-day snorkeling, $125.00; Lanai tour, $139.00; Molokini snorkeling tour $75.00. Children half-price on all tours.

Windjammer Maui. 505 Front St., Room 229, Lahaina; (808) 661-8600. 2½-hour whale-watching tours; also dinner cruises, with open bar, champagne, and live entertainment. Cost: whale-watching tour, $30.00; dinner cruise, $54.00 adults/$27.50 children; whale-watching tours $30.00 adults/$15.00 children.

Scuba Diving

Scuba diving is a popular recreational sport in Maui — especially around Molokini, just offshore from Maui — and at the nearby island of Lanai, with several different companies offering introductory scuba dives as well as tank dives for certified divers. Dives are offered both from the shore and from boats. Rates range from $35-$95 for introductory dives, and $40-$100 for tank dives; equipment is generally included.

Scuba Diving Outfitters and Operators. *Captain Nemo's Ocean Emporium,* 150 Dickenson St., Lahaina; (808) 661-5555. *Dive Maui,* Lahainaluna Rd., Lahaina; (808) 667-2080. *Lahaina Divers,* 710 Front St., Lahaina; (808) 667-4077. *Makena Coast Charters,* P.O. Box 1599, Kihei, HI 96753; (808) 874-1273. *Molokini Divers,* 1993 S. Kihei Rd., Kihei; (808) 879-0055. *Underwater Habitat,* Kihei; (808) 244-9739.

Sportfishing

There are more than a half-dozen companies offering sportfishing charters around Maui, operating primarily from Lahaina and Ma'alaea. Charters, typically, last 4-8 hours, with prices ranging from $60-$139 per person for shared or group charters, to $400-$700 for exclusive trips; rates include all equipment, as well as beverages on the trips. For more information, and reservations, contact any of the following: *Aerial Sportfishing Charters,* Lahaina, (808) 667-9089; *Carol Ann Charters,* Ma'alaea, (808) 877-2181; *Finest Kind Inc.,* Lahaina, (808) 661-0338; *Hinatea Sportfishing,* Lahaina, (808) 667-7548; *Lahaina Charter Boats,* Lahaina, (808) 667-6672; *Lucky Strike Charters,* Lahaina, (808) 661-4606; *Rascal Sportfishing Charters,* Ma'alaea, (808) 874-8633; or *West Maui Charters,* Lahaina, (808) 669-6193.

Windsurfing

Windsurfing is one of Maui's foremost recreational water sports, especially popular at Hookipa, near Paia, and off the coast of Kihei. Introductory lessons as well as sailboard rentals are available from several different local companies, with rates, typically, ranging from $50-$60 for lessons, to $250 for equipment rental for a week.

Windsurfing Outfitters and Operators. *Hawaiian Island Windsurfing,* 460 Dairy Rd., Kahului; (808) 572-5601/(800) 782-6105. *Hi-Tech Sailboards,* 444 Hana Hwy., Kahului; (808) 877-2111. *Maui Windsurfari,* 444 Hana Hwy., Kahului; (808) 871-7766. *Windsurfing West Maui,* 460 Dairy Rd., Kahului; (808) 871-8733.

Parasailing

Lahaina Para-sail. Lahaina Harbor, Lahaina; (808) 661-4887. Offers rides of around 10 minutes in the air. Cost: $48.00.

UFO Parasail. Whalers Village, Ka'anapali; (808) 661-7836. 10 minutes in the air. $50.00.

West Maui Para-sail. Lahaina; (808) 661-4060. 10-minute airborne rides; $48.00.

Waterskiing

Ka'anapali Water Ski. Ka'anapali; (808) 661-3324. Offers 15-, 30- and 60-minute waterskiing tows. Cost: 15-minute tow, $25.00; 30-minute tow, $50.00; 60-minute tow, $90.00. Reservations preferred.

Lahaina Waterski. Lahaina; (808) 661-5988. 15-, 30- and 60-minute tows available. Cost: 15-minute tow, $25.00; 30-minute tow, $50.00; 60-minute tow, $90.00. Call for reservations.

RESTAURANTS

(Restaurant prices — based on full course dinner, excluding drinks, tax and tips — are categorized as follows: *Deluxe*, over $30; *Expensive*, $20-$30; *Moderate*, $10-$20; *Inexpensive*, under $10.)

Lahaina and Ka'anapali

Alex's Hole in the Wall. *Moderate.* 834 Front St., Lahaina; (808) 661-3197. Traditional Italian cuisine, featuring pasta, veal and chicken dishes. Open for dinner. Reservations suggested.

Avalon. *Expensive.* 844 Front St., Lahaina; (808) 667-5559. Specializing in "Pacific Basin Cuisine," a blend of eastern and western cooking. Menu features fresh seafood, veal and poultry, served with a variety of tantalizing sauces. Lunch and dinner daily. Reservations recommended.

The Bay Club. *Expensive.* At the Kapalua Bay Hotel, One Bay Dr., Kapalua; (808) 669-5656. Well-appointed oceanview restaurant, offering guests some of the most breathtaking sunsets. Serves primarily fresh island seafood. Open for lunch and dinner. Reservations recommended.

The Beach Club. *Moderate.* At the Aston Ka'anapali Shores, 3445 Lower Honoapi'ilani Hwy., Ka'anapali; (808) 667-2211. Family-style restaurant in oceanfront setting. Continental cuisine, with emphasis on fresh seafood. Also live Hawaiian and contemporary music. Open for breakfast, lunch and dinner daily.

Buzz's Wharf. *Moderate.* Ma'alaea Bay; (808) 244-5426. Situated at the Ma'alaea Harbor, with superb views of the ocean, Kihei and Mt. Haleakala. Offers primarily fresh island seafood and steak. Lunch and dinner daily. Reservations suggested.

The Chart House. *Moderate.* 1450 Front St., Lahaina; (808) 661-0937. Established restaurant, quite popular with sunset-watchers. Specialties include fresh seafood, steak and prime rib. Open for dinner. Reservations suggested.

Chez Paul. *Expensive.* Hwy. 30, Olowalu Village; (808) 661-3843. One of the best-known French restaurants in Maui, offering classic French cuisine. Elegant decor. Dinners at 6.30 p.m. and 8.30 p.m. Reservations recommended.

Chico's Cantina. *Inexpensive.* In the Whaler's Village, Building G, 2435 Ka'anapali Pkwy., Ka'anapali; (808) 667-2777. Tropical Mexican restaurant, specializing in traditional south-of-the-border and southwestern cooking. Lunch and dinner daily.

Chopsticks. *Inexpensive.* At the Royal Lahaina Hotel, 2780 Kekaa Dr., (808) 661-3611. Asian and South Pacific cuisine. Good selection of dishes. Open for dinner daily.

Chris's Smokehouse. *Moderate-Expensive.* 1307 Front St., Lahaina; (808) 667-7005. Offers a good selection of smoked and charcoal broiled ribs, steaks, seafood and chicken. Open for lunch and dinner daily.

Compadres Mexican Bar & Grill. *Moderate.* The Cannery Mall, Lahaina; (808) 661-7189. Authentic Mexican food, including grilled fajitas and seafood entrees featuring fresh island fish. Breakfast, lunch and dinner daily.

Cooks on the Beach. *Inexpensive-Moderate.* At the Westin Maui, 2365 Ka'anapali Pkwy., (808) 667-2525. American cuisine, including prime rib buffet, served by the poolside. Hula show at 7 p.m. Open for breakfast, lunch and dinner; also brunch and late supper.

David Paul's Lahaina Grill. *Deluxe.* At the Lahaina Hotel. 127 Lahainaluna Rd., Lahaina; (808) 667-5117. Elegant restaurant, serving "New

American Cuisine," including European, Asian and southwestern dishes. Open for lunch and dinner. Reservations recommended.

Discovery Room. *Expensive-Deluxe.* At the Sheraton Maui Resort, 2605 Ka'anapali Pkwy., Ka'anapali; (808) 661-0031, ext. 5201. Specializing in Continental cuisine, with emphasis on seafood, steak and poultry. Live entertainment and dancing. Open for breakfast and dinner. Reservations recommended.

El Crab Catcher. *Moderate.* In the Whaler's Village, 2435 Ka'anapali Pkwy., Ka'anapali; (808) 661-4423. Located on Ka'anapali Beach, with panoramic views of the ocean. Menu features prime rib, fresh fish and other island specialties. Hawaiian music. Lunch and dinner daily. Reservations suggested.

Erik's Seafood Grotto. *Moderate.* 4242 Lower Honoapi'ilani Hwy., Kahana; (808) 669-4806. Located in the Kahana Villa condominium complex. Offers a wide selection of seafood dishes, including such delicacies as tiger prawns, stuffed with crabs, and a variety of fresh fish. Also steak, and Japanese menu. Open for dinner daily.

The Garden Restaurant. *Expensive.* At the Kapalua Bay Hotel, One Bay Dr., Kapalua; (808) 669-5656. Open-air setting, amid lush tropical plants and waterways. International cuisine. Open for breakfast and dinner, and Sunday brunch. Reservations recommended.

Gerard's Restaurant. *Expensive.* At the Plantation Inn, 174 Lahainaluna Rd., Lahaina; (808) 661-8939. French restaurant, serving fresh seafood and veal and lamb preparations. Entertainment. Open for lunch on Fridays, and dinner daily. Reservations suggested.

Golden Palace. *Moderate.* In the Lahaina Shopping Center, Lahaina; (808) 661-3126. Traditional Chinese cuisine. Offers full-course dinners as well as light lunches. Open for lunch and dinner daily. Reservations suggested.

The Grill. *Expensive.* One Ritz Carlton Dr., Kapalua; (808) 669-6200. Specializing in regional Hawaiian and Continental cuisine. Open for dinner daily; also Sunday brunch. Live jazz nightly.

The Harborfront. *Expensive.* Wharf Shopping Ctr., Front St., Lahaina; (808) 667-7822. Continental cuisine, with emphasis on fresh island seafood. Lunch and dinner daily. Reservations recommended.

Hard Rock Cafe. *Moderate.* 900 Front St., Lahaina; (808) 667-7400. Newer West Maui restaurant, decorated with rock 'n roll memorabilia. Serves primarily American fare. Open for lunch and dinner. Reservations suggested.

Juicy's. *Inexpensive.* 505 Front St., Suite 142, Lahaina; (808) 667-5727. Casual restaurant, featuring soups, salads, vegetarian dishes, and a variety of freshly-squeezed juices. Open daily; breakfast, lunch and dinner.

Kahana Keyes. *Moderate.* At the Valley Isle Resort, Kahana; (808) 669-8071. Oceanview restaurant. House specialties include seafood brochette, scampi, and barbecued baby back ribs. Live entertainment, and dancing. Open for dinner. Reservations suggested.

Kapalua Bay Club. *Expensive.* Kapalua Resort, One Bay Dr., Kapalua; (808) 669-8008. Open-air setting, with views of the islands of Molokai and Lanai. Serves fresh seafood, New York steak, and veal. Open for lunch and dinner. Reservations recommended.

Kapalua Grill & Bar. *Moderate.* 200 Kapalua Dr., Kapalua; (808) 669-5653. Features Continental cuisine, with emphasis on fresh island fish, lobster, steak, chicken and pasta. Superb views of West Maui Mountains and Napili Bay. Lunch and dinner daily. Reservations recommended.

Kau Kau Grill & Bar. *Inexpensive.* At the Maui Marriot Resort, 100 Nohea Kai Dr., Ka'anapali; (808) 667-1200, ext. 51. Poolside snack bar serving sandwiches, salads, burgers and cocktails. Open for breakfast and lunch.

Kimo's Restaurant. *Moderate.* 845 Front St., Lahaina; (808) 661-4811. Oceanfront setting; superb sunsets. Serves primarily fresh fish and prime rib. Open for lunch and dinner. Reservations suggested.

Kobe Japanese Steak House. *Expensive.* 136 Dickenson St., Lahaina; (808) 667-5555. Authentic Japanese cuisine, including Teppanyaki-style steak and seafood, prepared at the tableside. Also sushi bar. Open for dinner daily. Reservations recommended.

Lahaina Broiler. *Moderate.* 889 Front St., Lahaina; (808) 661-3111. Waterfront restaurant, offering good views of Kaho'olawe, Molokai and Lanai, and memorable sunsets. Menu features seafood, steak and prime rib. Open for breakfast, lunch and dinner.

Lahaina Coolers. *Inexpensive-Moderate.* 180 Dickenson St., Lahaina; (808) 661-7082. Hawaiian-style French bistro, with a unique bar, made from an 11-foot longboard. Features tropical pizzas, and a good selection of pasta dishes and salads. Open for breakfast, lunch and dinner daily.

Lahaina Provision Company. *Inexpensive-moderate.* At the Hyatt Regency Maui, Napili Tower, Ka'anapali; (808) 661-1234. Open-air setting. Serves primarily fresh island fish and steak. Also tropical luncheon buffet; and "chocoholic bar." Lunch and dinner daily. Reservations recommended

Leilani's on the Beach. *Moderate.* In the Whaler's Village, Building J, 2435 Ka'anapali Pkwy., Ka'anapali; (808) 661-4495. Open-air restaurant, situated on Ka'anapali Beach, with unobstructed views of the ocean. Offers seafood, steak, and chicken. Open for lunch and dinner. Reservations suggested.

Lokelani. *Moderate-Expensive.* At the Maui Marriott Resort, 100 Nohea Kai Dr., Ka'anapali; (808) 667-1200. Specializing in seafood, with emphasis on fresh local fish; also other island favorites. Extensive menu. Open for dinner. Reservations recommended.

Longhi's Restaurant. *Moderate-Expensive.* 888 Front St., Lahaina; (808) 667-2288. Traditional Italian cooking, featuring a variety of pasta dishes, veal, fresh fish, and steaks. Entertainment and dancing on weekends. Open for breakfast, lunch and dinner daily.

Luigi's. *Inexpensive-Moderate.* Ka'anapali Parkway, Ka'anapali; (808) 661-3160. Casual, family-style restaurant, serving gourmet pizza, seafood, pasta and vegetarian dishes. Open for lunch and dinner daily.

Marie Callender's Restaurant & Pie Shop. *Moderate.* In the Lahaina Cannery Shopping Center, 1221 Honoapi'ilani Hwy., Lahaina; (808) 667-7437. Freshly baked pies and pastries; also waffles, deli sandwiches, pasta, ribs, and other specialties. Breakfast, lunch and dinner daily.

The Market Cafe. *Moderate.* At The Shops at the Kapalua Bay Hotel, 115 Bay Dr., Kapalua; (808) 669-4888. Contemporary American fare, including sandwiches and pasta dishes. Casual atmosphere. Open for breakfast and lunch.

Moana Terrace. *Inexpensive-Moderate.* At the Maui Marriott Resort, 100 Nohea Kai Dr., Ka'anapali; (808) 667-1200. American cuisine, served in open-air setting. Lavish buffets. Breakfast, lunch and dinner daily. Reservations suggested.

Moose McGillycuddy's. *Inexpensive.* 844 Front St., Lahaina; (808) 667-7758. Popular local restaurant, featuring standard American fare, including chicken, steak, prime rib and seafood. Live entertainment. Open for breakfast, lunch and dinner daily.

Nanatomi. *Moderate.* At the Ka'anapali Beach Resort, Ka'anapali; (808) 667-7902. Authentic Japanese cuisine, emphasizing fresh island fish. Also sushi bar. Open for breakfast, lunch and dinner. Reservations suggested.

Nikko Steak House. *Expensive.* At the Maui Marriott, 100 Nohea Kai Dr., Ka'anapali; (808) 667-1200. Japanese steakhouse, featuring ancient art of Teppanyaki cooking. Open for dinner. Reservations recommended.

Ohana Bar & Grill. *Moderate.* At the Embassy Suites Resort, 104 Ka'anapali Shores Pl., Ka'anapali; (808) 661-2000. Casual poolside restaurant, overlooking the ocean. Features American cuisine primarily. Also fresh seafood, pasta and prime rib. Extensive wine list. Entertainment. Open for lunch and dinner daily.

Orient Express. *Moderate.* At Napili Shores Resort, Napili; (808) 669-8077. Thai and Chinese cuisine, featuring authentic Thai curries, and fresh seafood, poultry and pork preparations. Open for dinner, Tues.-Sun. Reservations recommended.

Papillion. *Expensive-Deluxe.* Kapalua Bay Hotel, One Bay Dr., Kapalua; (808) 669-6129. Outdoor, oceanview restaurant, overlooking lush gardens. International and Hawaiian cuisine. Open for breakfast daily, dinner Tues.-Sat.; also Sunday brunch, and seafood buffets on Friday nights. Reservations recommended.

Pavilion. *Moderate.* Hyatt Regency Maui, Ka'anapali; (808) 661-1234. Poolside dining; casual atmosphere. Serves primarily American cuisine. Also breakfast buffet daily. Open for breakfast and lunch.

Pineapple Hill Restaurant. *Inexpensive-Moderate.* 1000 Kapalua Dr., Kapalua; (808) 669-6129. Housed in old plantation-era house, offering guests some of the loveliest sunsets. Varied cuisine. Open for dinner daily. Reservations recommended.

Pioneer Inn Grill & Bar. *Moderate-Expensive.* 658 Wharf St., Lahaina; (808) 661-3636. Housed in the Pioneer Inn; overlooking Lahaina Harbor. American and Thai cuisine. Informal setting. Open for lunch and dinner daily.

Royal Ocean Terrace. *Inexpensive-Moderate.* At the Royal Lahaina Resort, 2780 Kekaa Dr., Ka'anapali; (808) 661-3611, ext. 2244. Standard American fare. Also breakfast buffets and Sunday brunch. Open for breakfast, lunch and dinner. Reservations suggested.

Scaroles Italian Ristorante & Pizzeria. *Moderate.* 930 Wainee St., Lahaina; (808) 661-4466. Authentic Italian cuisine, including pasta, veal, chicken, seafood, and eggplant; also New York-style thin-crust pizza. Open for lunch and dinner.

The Sea House Restaurant. *Moderate.* At the Napili Kai Beach Club, 5900 Honoapi'ilani Rd., Napili; (808) 669-1500. Delightful setting, overlooking Napili Bay. Specialties here are rack of lamb and fresh island seafood. Live Hawaiian entertainment, and dancing. Breakfast, lunch and dinner daily. Reservations recommended.

Sound of the Falls. *Expensive.* At The Westin Maui, 2365 Ka'anapali Pkwy., Ka'anapali; (808) 667-2525. Pacific Rim cuisine, served in delightful setting. Entertainment and dancing. Open for dinner. Reservations recommended.

Spat's. *Moderate.* At the Hyatt Regency Maui, Atrium Tower, 200 Nohea Kai Dr., Ka'anapali; (808) 661-1234. Traditional Northern Italian and Mediterranean cuisine. Dancing after 10 p.m. Open for dinner daily. Reservations recommended.

Swan Court. *Expensive-Deluxe.* At the Hyatt Regency Maui, 200 Nohea Kai Dr., Ka'anapali; (808) 661-1234. Oceanfront setting, surrounded by waterfalls and a swan pond; acknowledged as one of the ten most romantic restaurants in the world. Gourmet cuisine. Open for breakfast and dinner. Reservations recommended.

Tasca Ristorante & Spirits. *Moderate-Expensive.* 608 Front St., Lahaina; (808) 661-8001. Extensive menu, featuring Mediterranean cuisine, including escargot and broiled ahi; also baby back ribs. Open for lunch and dinner. Reservations suggested.

The Terrace. *Expensive.* At the Ritz-Carlton Resort, One Ritz-Carlton Dr., Kapalua; (808) 669-6200. Features Pacific Rim cuisine, and seafood buffets on Fridays. Live Hawaiian entertainment. Open for dinner. Reservations recommended.

Thai Chef Restaurant. *Inexpensive.* Lahaina Shopping Ctr., Lahaina; (808) 667-2814. Authentic Thai food, with a complete vegetarian menu. Open for lunch and dinner.

Tiki Terrace. *Moderate.* At the Ka'anapali Beach Hotel, Ka'anapali; (808) 661-0011. Garden restaurant, serving Continental and Hawaiian cuisine, with emphasis on fresh seafood, chicken and beef. Hawaiian entertainment, including hula dancers. Open for dinner daily. Reservations recommended.

The Villa. *Moderate.* At The Westin Maui, 2365 Ka'anapali Pkwy., Ka'anapali; (808) 667-2525. Seafood and pasta dishes; also seafood buffet. Hawaiian entertainment. Open for dinner. Reservations suggested.

Kihei - Makena

Cabana Cafe. *Inexpensive.* At the Four Season's Resort, 3900 Wailea Alanui, Wailea; (808) 874-8000. Casual, poolside cafe, serving hamburgers, sandwiches and salads. Lunch and dinner daily.

Cafe Kiowai. *Inexpensive-Moderate.* At the Maui Prince Hotel, 5400 Makena Alanui, Makena; (808) 874-1111. Continental cuisine, featuring fresh seafood, prime rib and pasta dishes. Open-air setting, casual atmosphere; overlooking garden and koi ponds. Open for breakfast, lunch an dinner. Reservations suggested.

Canton Chef. *Moderate.* Kamaole Shopping Center, Kihei; (808) 879-1988. Chinese cuisine, emphasizing seasonal, fresh food, prepared with a variety of spices. Open for lunch and dinner. Reservations recommended.

Carelli's on the Beach. *Moderate.* At the Wailea Beachfront Hotel, 2980 S. Kihei Rd., Kihei; (808) 875-0001. Traditional Italian cuisine, featuring a variety of pasta dishes and freshly-baked pizzas, prepared in wood-burning ovens. Also seafood bar. Open for dinner daily. Reservations suggested.

Chuck's Steak House. *Moderate.* Kihei Town Center, across from Kalama Park, Kihei; (808) 879-4488. Menu features steak, fresh fish, lobster and prime rib. Also salad bar. Open for lunch and dinner. Reservations recommended.

Erik's Seafood Broiler. *Moderate.* Kamaole Shopping Center, 2463 S. Kihei Rd., Kihei; (808) 879-8400. House specialties are fresh island fish and rack of lamb; also broiled lobster tail, king crab legs and porterhouse steak. Casual setting; beautiful sunsets. Open for dinner.

Fairway Restaurant. *Moderate.* At the Wailea Golf Course, 100 Kaukahi St., Wailea; (808) 879-4060. Oceanview restaurant, serving Continental cuisine. Specialties are filet mignon and veal parmigiana. Open for breakfast, lunch and dinner. Reservations suggested.

Ferrari's. *Moderate.* 1945 S. Kihei Rd., Kihei; (808) 879-1535. Well-appointed restaurant. Specialties here are homemade pasta, fresh fish and other seafood, and pizza. Reservations recommended.

Hakone. *Expensive.* At the Maui Prince Hotel, 5400 Makena Alanui, Makena; (808) 874-1111. Authentic Japanese cuisine, prepared in a variety of styles. Also sushi bar. Open for dinner daily. Reservations recommended.

Hula Moons. *Moderate-Expensive.* At the Maui Inter-Continental Resort, 3700 Wailea Alanui Dr., Wailea; (808) 879-1922. Oceanfront restaurant, specializing in fresh island seafood. Extensive salad bar. Live entertainment. Open for lunch and dinner daily.

Humuhumunukunukuapua'a. *Expensive.* At the Grand Wailea Resort, 3850 Wailea Alanui Dr., Wailea; (808) 875-1234. Authentic thatched-roof restaurant, situated beside lagoon. Serves primarily Hawaiian cuisine, with emphasis on fresh local seafood. Open for dinner daily. Reservations recommended.

Island Fish House. *Moderate.* 1945 S. Kihei Rd., Kihei; (808) 879-7771. Good selection of fresh local catch; also New York steak and beef and chicken dishes. Open for dinner. Reservations suggested.

Kihei Prime Rib and Seafood House. *Moderate.* 2511 S. Kihei Rd., Kihei; (808) 879-1954. Specializing in prime rib and seafood. Spectacular views of the islands of Lanai, Kaho'olawe and Molokini; memorable sunsets. Open for dinner daily. Reservations suggested.

Lanai Terrace. *Moderate.* At the Maui Inter-Continental Resort, 3700 Wailea Alanui, Wailea; (808) 879-1922. Oceanview restaurant, in open-air setting. Offers contemporary American cuisine, and lavish buffets. Breakfast and lunch daily. Reservations suggested.

Maui Onion. *Moderate.* At Stouffer's Wailea Beach Resort. 3550 Wailea Alanui, Wailea; (808) 879-4900, ext. 7829. Informal, poolside setting. House specialties are Maui onion rings and tropical fruit smoothies. Open for lunch daily.

Ocean Terrace. *Moderate.* At Mana Kai Maui Hotel, 2960 S. Kihei Rd., Kihei; (808) 879-2607. Open-air setting; outstanding ocean views. Serves primarily Continental cuisine, including steak, scampi, chicken teriyaki, and fettucine; also fresh, homemade bread. Open for breakfast, lunch and dinner.

Pacific Grill. *Moderate.* At the Four Seasons Resort, 3900 Wailea Alanui Dr., Wailea; (808) 874-8000. Specializing in Pacific Rim cuisine. Lavish buffets. Breakfast, lunch and dinner daily. Reservations recommended.

Palm Court. *Moderate.* At Stouffer's Wailea Beach Resort, 3550 Wailea Alanui Dr., Wailea; (808) 879-4900. Overlooking lush tropical gardens; open-air setting. Features champagne breakfast buffets, and also dinner buffets. Open for breakfast and dinner daily.

Prince Court. *Deluxe.* At the Maui Prince Hotel, 5400 Makena Alanui, Makena; (808) 874-1111. Elegant, oceanview restaurant, serving Continental cuisine. Menu emphasizes island-inspired dishes. Extensive wine list. Entertainment. Open for dinner. Reservations recommended.

Raffles. *Deluxe.* At Stouffer's Wailea Beach Resort, 3550 Wailea Alanui Dr., Wailea; (808) 879-4900. Award-winning gourmet restaurant, specializing in Continental cuisine. Specialties are rack of lamb, and souffles for dessert. Entertainment. Open for dinner. Reservations recommended.

Restaurant Isana Shogun. *Moderate.* 515 S. Kihei Rd., Kihei; (808) 874-5034. Authentic, teppan-style Japanese cuisine, featuring Hawaiian lobster tail, chicken teriyaki, and steaks; also sushi bar. Open for dinner. Reservations suggested.

Sandcastle Restaurant. *Moderate.* Wailea Shopping Village, Wailea; (808) 879-0606. Serves fresh seafood, including locally caught mahi mahi, and steaks and prime rib. Also salad bar. Open for breakfast, lunch and dinner. Reservations suggested.

Seasons. *Expensive.* At the Four Seasons Resort, 3900 Wailea Alanui Dr., Wailea; (808) 874-8000. Elegant, well-regarded restaurant, serving California cuisine and fresh island seafood. Entertainment. Open for dinner. Jackets required; reservations recommended.

Central Maui

Mama's Fish House. *Moderate-Expensive.* 799 Poho Pl., Kuau; (808) 579-8488. Popular Maui restaurant, situated on the beach at Kuau Cove, just east of Paia. Menu features fresh island seafood, including lobster and shrimp, and beef preparations. Open for lunch and dinner. Reservations recommended.

Ming Yuen. *Inexpensive.* 162 Alamaha St., Kahului; (808) 871-7787. Cantonese and Szechuan cuisine. Varied menu. Open for lunch and dinner.

Picnics Restaurant. *Inexpensive.* Baldwin Ave., Paia, (808) 579-8021. Offers picnic baskets with roast meats, freshly-baked breads, salads, and desserts. Also cappuccino, and homemade muffins and pastries. Open daily.

Saeng's Thai Cuisine. *Moderate.* 2119 Vineyard St., Wailuku; (808) 244-1567. Good selection of Thai food, including appetizers, soups and salads. Entrees include seafood specialties, and curried chicken, beef and pork, prepared in a variety of styles; also several vegetarian dishes. Dinner daily. Reservations suggested.

Siam Thai Cuisine. *Inexpensive-Moderate.* 123 N. Market St., Wailuku; (808) 244-3817. Popular local restaurant, serving authentic Thai food, including such dishes as Evil Prince Chicken, ginger beef, and shrimp sateh. Food prepared to suit individual taste — mild, medium or hot. Open for dinner daily, lunch Mon.-Fri.

Tropical Restaurant. *Moderate.* At the Maui Tropical Plantation, on Honoapi'ilani Hwy., Waikapu; (808) 244-7643. A favorite with visitors to Maui. Offers tropical buffets and locally-grown fruit and nuts. Hawaiian country entertainment. Open for breakfast, lunch and dinner daily. Reservations recommended.

The Vegan Restaurant. *Inexpensive.* 115 Baldwin Ave., Paia; (808) 579-9144. A wholly vegetarian restaurant, offering a variety of dishes without cholesterol. Also fresh salads, vegetarian burgers, and fruit smoothies. Casual atmosphere. Open daily.

Wolfgang's Bistro Garden. *Moderate-Expensive.* 33 Lono Ave., Kahului; (808) 871-7555. Informal restaurant, specializing in Continental and German cuisine. Also offers steaks and seafood, and poultry and pasta dishes. Open for lunch Mon.-Fri., dinner Tues.-Sat.

Upcountry and Hana

Casanova Italian Restaurant & Deli. *Inexpensive-Moderate.* 1188 Makawao Ave., Makawao; (808) 572-0220. Traditional, home-style Italian cooking, featuring lasagna, homemade pasta and seafood dishes; also salads, and pizzas baked in a wood-burning oven. Entertainment. Open for dinner. Reservations suggested.

Fu Wah Chinese Restaurant. *Inexpensive-Moderate.* Pukalani Terrace Center, 55 Pukalani St., Pukalani; (808) 572-1341. Authentic Cantonese and Szechuan cuisine. House specialties are lobster with black bean sauce, and fresh fish with ginger and onion sauce. Open for lunch and dinner.

Haliimaile General Store. *Moderate.* 900 Haliimaile Rd., Haliimaile; (808) 572-2666. Specializing in traditional American cuisine. Homemade entrees and desserts. Country store setting. Lunch and dinner daily.

Hana Ranch Restaurant. *Moderate.* At the Hotel Hana-Maui, Hana Hwy., Hana; (808) 248-8255. Steaks and seafood on weekends; pizza on Thursday nights. Open for dinner Thurs.-Sat. Reservations recommended.

Kula Lodge & Restaurant. *Moderate.* Haleakala Hwy. (377), Kula; (808) 878-1535. Contemporary Pacific Rim cuisine. Superb views of Central and West Maui. Open for breakfast, lunch and dinner. Reservations recommended.

Makawao Steak House. *Moderate.* 3612 Baldwin Ave., Makawao; (808) 572-8711. Established Makawao restaurant, noted for its steaks and seafood. Casual atmosphere. Open for dinner and Sunday brunch.

Polli's Mexican Cantina. *Inexpensive-moderate.* 1202 Makawao Ave.,

Makawao; (808) 572-7808. Casual family restaurant, serving authentic Mexican food and drinks. Entertainment. Open for lunch and dinner.

Tutu's at Hana Bay. *Inexpensive.* Keawa Pl., Hana; (808) 248-8224. Popular local eatery, located at the Hana Beach Park at Hana Bay. Offers sandwiches and burgers primarily.

LUAUS

(Prices for traditional Hawaiian luaus range, typically, from $40-$50 for adults to $20-$25 for children.)

Drums of the Pacific Luau. At the Sunset Terrace at Hyatt Regency Maui, Ka'anapali; (808) 661-1234. All-you-can-eat buffets, featuring traditional Hawaiian dishes. Entertaining Polynesian shows. Luau dinners on Mon., Wed., Fri. and Sat. Reservations recommended.

Luau at Sheraton Maui. At the Sheraton Maui, Ka'anapali; (808) 661-3500. Beachfront setting; Polynesian buffets. Entertainment features traditional songs and dances of Hawaii, Tahiti, Samoa and New Zealand. Luaus every night. Reservations suggested.

Maui Lu Resort Luau. At the Maui Lu Resort, 575 S. Kihei Rd., Kihei; (808) 879-5858. Luau dinners begin with the traditional imu ceremony, featuring the removal of the kalua pig from the earthen oven. Lavish Polynesian buffet, followed by a Polynesian show. Luaus every Tuesday and Saturday night. Reservations recommended.

Luau at Maui Inter-Continental Resort. At the Maui Inter-Continental Resort, 3700 Wailea Alanui, Wailea; (808) 879-1922. Imu ceremony at sunset, followed by traditional Hawaiian buffet, and Polynesian revue. Luaus on Tues., Thurs. and Fri. Reservations recommended.

Maui Marriott Luau. Held at the Maui Marriott, Ka'anapali; (808) 661-5828. Authentic Hawaiian luau; begins with a lei greeting ceremony, and features a buffet consisting of kalua pig, Hawaiian sweet potatoes and poi. Also Polynesian show, with songs and dances of the islands. Luaus every night. Reservations suggested.

Old Lahaina Luau. 505 Front St., Lahaina; (808) 667-1998/(800) 248-5828. Traditional Hawaiian buffet; features kalua roast pork, teriyaki steak, and mahi mahi, among other foods. Live music, and hula. Luau on Tuesdays and Saturdays. Reservations recommended.

Royal Lahaina Luau. At the Luau Gardens at the Royal Lahaina Hotel, Ka'anapali; (808) 661-3611, ext. 2340. Hawaiian and Polynesian foods. Live entertainment. Luaus offered every night. Reservations recommended

Stouffer's Wailea Beach Resort Luau. At Stouffer's Wailea Beach Resort, 3550 Wailea Alanui, Wailea; (808) 879-4900. Oceanfront setting. Luau begins with imu ceremony, followed by lavish Polynesian buffet. Also Polynesian show. Luau dinners on Mondays and Thursdays. Reservations recommended.

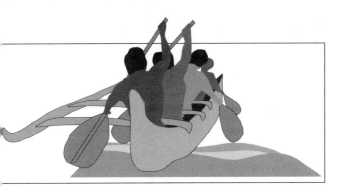

MOLOKAI

"The Friendly Isle"

Molokai is Hawaii's "Friendly Isle" — for the outdoorsman, adventurer, nature lover. It was one of the first of the Hawaiian islands to be inhabited, yet remains largely untouched by the rigors of development, with only one small resort, Kaluakoi, near the northwest corner of the island. It also offers great variety — ideal, again, for the outdoor enthusiast — from the lush, green Halawa Valley in the east to the arid slopes of the Maunaloa mountain in the west, from the friendly, natural harbors along the southeast shore, at Kaunakakai and Kamalo, to the isolated, yet beautiful, Kalaupapa Peninsula at the north end of the island, situated at the bottom of 2,000-foot-high sea cliffs. Besides which, the island also boasts some of the best, uncluttered beaches in Hawaii — on its west coast — as well as hiking trails through a pristine, nature wonderland, the 2,774-acre Kamakou Preserve.

Molokai is the fifth largest island in the Hawaiian chain, some 38 miles long and 10 miles wide, more or less rectangle- or slipper-shaped. It comprises, primarily, two land masses — East Molokai and West Molokai — created by the volcanoes, Mt. Kamakou (elevation, 4,970 feet) and Maunaloa (elevation, 1,381 feet), respectively, and joined together by a dry plain, which makes up Central Molokai. In East Molokai are the ancient Halawa Valley and Molokai's principal population center, Kaunakakai; in West Molokai lie the town of Maunaloa — birthplace of the hula — and the Kaluakoi Resort; and in Central Molokai, the community of Hoolehua and a macadamia nut farm that welcomes visitors. A separate tour takes in the remote Kalaupapa Peninsula, at the north end of the island.

Molokai is situated roughly 9 miles north of Lanai, or 8½ miles northwest of Maui; from Oahu, it is approximately 25 miles distant, lying just to the southeast. The island can be reached by ferry from Maui, or on inter-island flights from Maui, Lanai or Oahu. Molokai's main airport, the Molokai Airport, is located at Hoolehua, in Central Molokai.

MOLOKAI

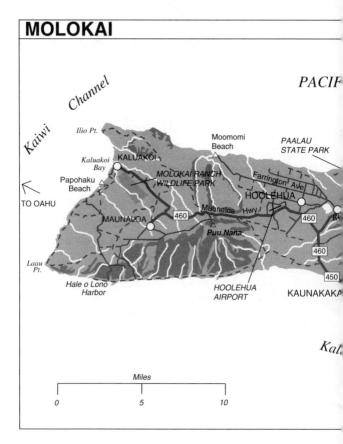

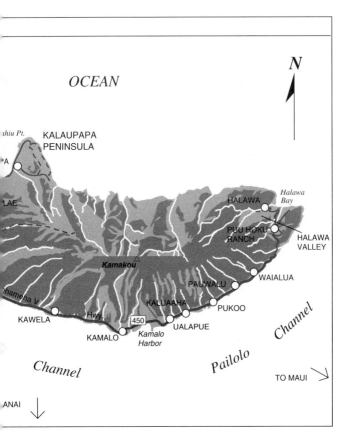

Kaunakakai

Kaunakakai is Molokai's principal town, and an ideal base from which to explore the rest of the island. It is situated on the south coast of the island, some 7 miles southeast of the Molokai Airport in Hoolehua, more or less equidistant from the remote east and west coasts of the island. It also has in it most of the island's shops, restaurants and other amenities, including a handful of deli-cum-markets and local eateries, a gift shop, a sporting goods store, an art gallery, and even a bakery, the Kanemitsu Bakery, which sells freshly-baked "Molokai Bread" — all strung along a three-block section of the town's main street, Ala Malama. The town, besides, has some good accommodations — the Pau Hana Inn and Molokai Hotel, both modest hotels with dining facilities, entertainment, and swimming pools, situated just to the south of the Kamehameha V Highway (450), fronting on the ocean; and Molokai Shores, a condominium complex, and a relatively new addition to Kaunakakai's accommodations, also oceanfront, situated just off the highway.

Kaunakakai also has a notable harbor, the Kaunakakai Harbor — Molokai's only deep-water port — located just to the southwest of town, off Kaunakakai Road. The Kaunakakai Harbor originally provided a landing for early-day canoes, when native Hawaiians journeyed here for the plentiful fish found in the area; it is, however, now a commercial port, where ferries and commuter boats to and from the neighboring island of Maui depart and arrive, and from where the island's honey, cattle, watermelons and other produce are shipped. The harbor is also home to fishing and charter boats, with some of them offering deep-sea fishing, diving, snorkeling, and even whale-watching excursions.

Kaunakakai, we might add, also has its associations with King Kamehameha V, ruler of Hawaii, who once maintained a vacation home here, the platform of which can still be seen, located near the beach, on the west side of Kaunakakai Road, just above the wharf. Interestingly, the beach fronting the Kamehameha home site was once used exclusively by the *ali'i* — or chiefs — for sunbathing.

Of interest, too, a mile or so west of the center of Kaunakakai, off the highway (460), is Kapuaiwa, one of the last surviving royal coconut groves on the island, planted in the 1860s for Kamehameha V; and directly across from there, on the opposite side of the highway, is Church Row, with its small section of quaint, box-like churches — one for almost every denomination.

From Kaunakakai, of course, the Kamehameha V Highway (450) journeys east along the coast to the Halawa Valley, and the Maunaloa Highway (460) heads out northwestward to the town of Maunaloa, and farther to the remote west coast of the island. From Kaunakakai, too, you can explore Central Molokai, just to the north, or continue farther, northward on Highways 460 and 470, to the sea cliffs above Kalaupapa.

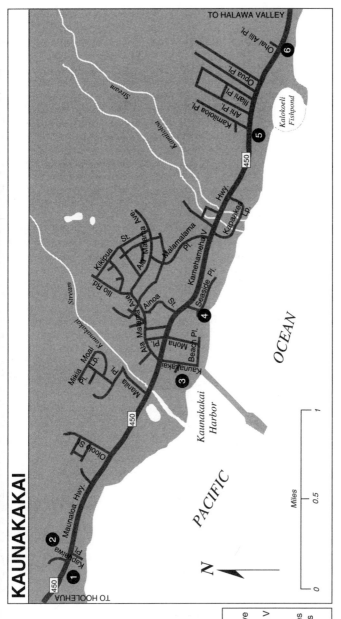

KAUNAKAKAI

1. Kapuaiwa
   Coconut Grove
2. Church Row
3. Kamehameha V
   Homesite
4. Pau Hana Inn
5. Molokai Shores
   Condominiums
6. Hotel Molokai

East Molokai

East Molokai, for the purposes of our tour, comprises largely the area extending eastward from Kaunakakai, some 30 miles, along the southeast coast of the island, to the Halawa Valley. The area, of course, was once the most densely populated on the island, dotted with more than 50 fishponds — an ancient form of Hawaiian aquaculture — many of them dating from the 13th century, the remnants of some of which can still be seen along the coast here, mainly between Kaunakakai and Puko'o. Typically, a fishpond consisted of a narrow, encircling or straight wall, built from stone or coral, connecting two points of the shore, with small openings placed at intervals in the wall, to allow the water to circulate. The pond was then stocked with fish, which were harvested as needed. A good example of this early form of Hawaiian ingenuity is the Kaloko'eli Fishpond, located directly behind the Molokai Shores condominiums, a little over a mile from the center of Kaunakakai. Another fishpond, easily viewed, is the Ali'i Fishpond, near the Oneali'i Beach Park, off the highway (450), some 3 miles from Kaunakakai.

In any event, East Molokai, besides its fishponds, has more to offer the visitor. Some 5 or 6 miles from Kaunakakai, for instance, eastward on the Kamehameha V Highway (450), lies Kawela, a small village, notable as the site of King Kamehameha I's invasion of Molokai in the late 1700s, in which Kamehameha defeated and conquered the island, in his quest for domination over all the Hawaiian islands. At Kawela, too, just off the highway, are the Kakahai'a Beach Park and National Wildlife Refuge, the latter a sanctuary for rare endemic birds. Another place of note here is a *pu'ukaua* — or fortress — which served as a place of refuge for those escaping capture or death. The *pu'ukaua*, however, is situated in the steep Kawela Gulch, and is virtually inaccessible to most visitors.

Another 4 miles or so — 10 miles east of Kaunakakai — and we are at Kamalo, one of Molokai's few natural harbors, which, before the island's commerce was diverted to Kaunakakai, was an important landing spot for canoes, and even small ships. At Kamalo, too, you can search out the small, wood-frame St. Joseph Church, built by Father Damien in 1876, located on the *makai* side of the highway, three-quarters of a mile past mile marker 10. There is a statue of Father Damien at the front of the church.

A mile or so past the St. Joseph Church in Kamalo, alongside Highway 450, is the site of the Smith and Bronte Landing, where, on July 14, 1927, as students of aviation history will recall, Ernest Smith and Emory Bronte crash-landed their airplane, upon successful completion of their historic flight from California — the first civilian transpacific flight — which took all of $25\frac{1}{2}$ hours. The site of the landing, now overgrown with brush and *kiawe* trees, is marked with a wooden sign.

Farther still, another mile or so — at mile marker 13 — lies the village of Ualapu'e, which has in it a general store, and the ocean-front Wavecrest Condominiums, with rental units, a swimming pool and tennis courts; and one and one-half miles east of there is Kalua'aha, another small village, which, at one time, was the chief population center of Molokai. In Kalua'aha, of course, you can visit the Kalua'aha Church, the oldest Christian church on Molokai, and, quite possibly, also one of the largest western-style churches on the islands, built in 1844 by Reverend Harvey Hitchcock and his wife, who, incidentally, were the first Protestant missionaries to arrive in Kalua'aha.

Nearby, too, a little to the east of the Kalua'aha Church, and also worth visiting, is Our Lady of Sorrows Church, another church built by Father Damien. The wood-frame church was originally built in 1874, and rebuilt in 1966.

Also of interest, three quarters of a mile farther, is the Ili'iliopae Heiau, Molokai's oldest and largest *heiau* (temple), reached by way of a foot trail which goes north off the highway, briefly, crossing over a creek bed, to the base of the *heiau*. The *heiau* — which, according to local lore, was built in a single night, by Hawaii's legendary *menehune* people, who carried the stones for the building from the ocean near the Wailau Valley, over the mountains, some 7 miles! — has an 87-foot-wide and 286-foot-long platform, which, originally, is believed to have been nearly 920 feet long. The *heiau*, however, we must point out, is located on private property, and permission must be obtained, from Destination Molokai Association, by calling (808) 553-3876; alternatively, you can arrange to tour the *heiau* with Molokai Trail and Wagon Ride (808-558-8380), who also tour the lush, surrounding countryside, including a visit to one of the world's largest mango groves.

In any case, the Ili'iliopae Heiau, besides being a place of worship, was once also a site for human sacrifices, and legend has it that a man once lived in the vicinity of the *heiau*, who had ten sons, nine of whom were sacrificed at the *heiau* by evil priests. Seeking to avenge the sacrifices, he sought out Kauhuhu, the shark god, who dwelled in a cave along Molokai's north coast. Kauhuhu agreed to avenge the deaths of the man's sons, and sent a flood of water through the valley, destroying the *heiau* and washing the evil priests out to sea, where, quite appropriately, they were eaten up by sharks

A little way from the Ili'iliopae Heiau, however, a half mile or so — some 16 miles east of Kaunakakai — lies Puko'o, which, during the 1900s, before the ascendancy of Kaunakakai as Molokai's commercial hub, was the seat of the island's government, with a courthouse, jail, and a hotel located there. Puko'o is now a sleepy little village, with only a small grocery store and snack bar. It is, nevertheless, also the last place to replenish supplies before journeying farther east, to the Halawa Valley.

Eastward still, some 4 miles, just before mile marker 20, on the *mauka* — inland — side of the highway, you can see the ruins of the Moanui Sugar Mill, originally built in the 1870s by plantation owner E. Baldwin, and destroyed by fire, some years later, in the 1880s; and just to the east of there, another quarter mile, at mile marker 20, is the Murphey's Beach Park — a small, sandy beach, protected by a reef, and with good picnicking and swimming possibilities. The beach, incidentally, is named for George Murphey, former owner of the Pu'u O Hoku Ranch, and who, in fact, deeded the land for the park to the state. There are good views of Maui from here, across the Pailolo Channel, and also of Kanaha Rock and Moku Ho'oniki Island — both bird sanctuaries, and the latter also the site of a bombing range during World War II — just to the northeast.

A mile past Murphey's Beach, where the road turns sharply to the left, around a huge rock, is Rock Point, one of Molokai's only surf breaks; and a little farther, past mile marker 22, after the highway begins to head inland, climbing, northward, lies the Pu'u O Hoku Ranch, with its green pastures, dotted with grazing horses. The Pu'u O Hoku Ranch, of course, was once owned by millionaire Paul Fagan, who later moved from Molokai to Hana, Maui, where he established the celebrated Hana Ranch. Interestingly, too, a famous prophet of Molokai, Lanikaula, is buried at the Pu'u O Hoku Ranch, in a sacred *kukui* grove. Lanikaula, we are told, lived on the eastern part of the island during the latter part of the 16th century, and his fame is largely derived from a momentous occasion, when the king of Maui, Kamalalwalu, was preparing to invade the nearby island of Hawaii, and all the other prophets and priests offered the king flattering prophecies, while Lanikaula warned Kamalalwalu of imminent danger in the battle. Kamalalwalu, needless to say, was rather displeased with Lanikaula, and vowed to kill him upon his return. However, as it turned out, Kamalalwalu was slain in battle on Hawaii, true to Lanikaula's prophecy, and his vow to put Lanikaula to death was left unfulfilled.

In any event, beyond the Pu'u O Hoku Ranch, the highway begins its descent, into the lush, green Halawa Valley, passing by an overlook, roughly a mile past mile marker 25, from where you can view the picturesque Moa'ula and Hipuapua falls, cascading hundreds of feet down the verdant hills above the valley; and a mile farther — some 27 miles east of Kaunakakai — the highway (450) finally ends, in the Halawa Valley, site of the first recorded settlement on Molokai, dating from 650 A.D. The Halawa Valley, in fact, was once inhabited by hundreds of families, and covered with *taro* patches, supplying much of the island with its *taro*, the Hawaiian staple. Indeed, as late as 1836, the population of Halawa Valley was around 500. However, in 1946, a *tsunami* — tidal wave — devoured much of the valley — farms and dwellings — and only a handful of families returned in the following years to live in the valley.

In the Halawa Valley, of course, at the end of the highway lies the Halawa Beach Park, situated along the Halawa Bay, at the mouth of the Halawa River, and frequented, primarily, by fishermen and vacationing families. Interestingly, the Halawa Bay was once also a well-regarded surfing spot, where the island's chiefs practiced the sport; and it continues to attract dedicated surfers even today.

The Halawa Valley's main attractions, however — and few, if any, would argue otherwise — are the Moa'ula and Hipuapua waterfalls, 250 feet and 500 feet high, respectively. The first of these, the Moa'ula Falls, can be reached by way of a 2½-mile trail that dashes off the highway (450), westward, roughly a quarter mile south of the

Halawa Beach Park, passing by rows of banana, papaya and guava trees. A quarter mile or so from the highway turnoff, the trail crosses over two streams and heads north, alongside another freshwater stream, some 2 miles, to the foot of the waterfalls, where there is a refreshing, natural pool, ideal for swimming. But a word of caution: in this icy pool, according to ancient legend, lives a *mo'o* — or lizard — and visitors must seek its permission before plunging in: drop a *ti* leaf into the pool; if it floats, you may enjoy the pool without further ado; if not, beware, danger lurks!

At any rate, there are also trails leading to the Upper Moa'ula and Hipuapua falls, more difficult than the Moa'ula Falls trail, but well worth the effort, especially for outdoor enthusiasts. Both trails branch off the Moa'ula Falls trail, a hundred yards or so before reaching the Moa'ula Falls. The Upper Moa'ula Falls trail, however, we must point out, is especially treacherous, narrowing at one point to a mere ledge along a sheer mountainside, with only a cable, bolted into the side of the mountain, for support. The trail, of course, goes west off the Moa'ula Falls trail; and the pool at the base of the waterfalls, needless to say, offers a degree of solitude unattainable elsewhere, with picnicking and swimming, besides. There are also spectacular views of the valley below, tumbling down toward the ocean.

The Hipuapua Falls trail, however, is not quite as difficult or hair-raising as the one leading to the Upper Moa'ula Falls, but neither is it easy to find, covered with rocks and foliage, and seldom trodden. Nevertheless, for the persevering types, we suggest hiking down from the Moa'ula Falls trail, past the Upper Moa'ula Falls trail turnoff, to the Hipuapua Stream, and following it upstream more or less directly to the falls. The Hipuapua Falls are magnificent, 500-foot waterfalls, where few, if any, venture, leaving it for the fortunate few to enjoy.

West Molokai

West Molokai lies largely between the 1,381-foot Pu'u Nana peak and the ocean, on the slopes of the volcanic Maunaloa mountain. It comprises, for the most part, dry, arid land, with Maunaloa, situated more or less at the center of West Molokai, as its chief town. It is also, we might add, notable as the birthplace of the *hula*, the traditional Hawaiian dance, and where, according to local lore, the goddess Laka learned the dance from her sister, Kapo, then traveled to all the other islands, teaching this traditional dance of storytelling.

Maunaloa itself is a small, rustic, one-road town, formerly a plantation town, built in 1923 by Libby, McNeil & Libby, to house the company's pineapple plantation workers, and located some 17 miles west of Kaunakakai, at the end of the Maunaloa Highway (460). The town has a general store, one or two eateries, and a handful of interesting little shops, notable among them, approximately at the center of town, the Big Wind Kite Factory, with its assortment of colorful, handcrafted kites, and where the staff also offer factory tours and kite flying lessons, besides. Worth visiting, too, adjacent to the Big Wind Kite Factory, is Jojo's Cafe, a popular, local eatery, which has in it an antique wooden bar. Jojo's, typically, serves hamburgers, hot dogs, fish, and soup, including a Hawaiian noodle soup and a hearty Portuguese bean soup.

West Molokai, we must also point out, is largely owned by the Molokai Ranch Company, the island's largest landholder, which owns more than 60,000 acres here, devoted primarily to cattle ranching. This, however, in all fairness, also has its negative aspect: access to the public beaches on the west and southwest part of the island — of which there are a handful — is restricted, with permission required from the company, incurring fees and deposits, at least a week in advance. For detailed information, we suggest you call the company at (808) 552-2741.

Here, too, at the Molokai Ranch, is the Molokai Ranch Wildlife Park, a 1,000-acre, African safari-type wild animal park, where more than 800 exotic animals, mainly African and Asian, roam freely — including giraffes, barbary sheep, greater kudu, oryx, sable antelope, rhea, eland and zebra — which can be seen on guided, $1\frac{1}{2}$-hour van tours of the park, departing from the nearby Kaluakoi Resort. It is, however, advisable to call ahead for tour reservations, at (808) 552-2741.

Kaluakoi

The Kaluakoi Resort is situated along a stretch of white-sand beach on the island's northwest shore, reached on Kaluakoi Road, which goes off the Maunaloa Highway (450), some 15 miles west of Kaunakakai. Kaluakoi is in fact Molokai's only resort development, with a single hotel, the Kaluakoi Hotel and Golf Club, formerly the Sheraton Molokai, originally developed in 1977. The hotel consists primarily of two-story redwood structures, with 290 guest rooms — most with ocean views — fronting on Kepuhi Beach, a long, sandy beach, with some swimming possibilities in the summer months, when the ocean is calm. The hotel has two well-appointed restaurants, a freshwater swimming pool, tennis courts, and an 18-hole, championship golf course. There are also two condominium developments here, Ke Nani Kai and the 77-unit Paniolo Hale, the latter with private lanais with hot tubs, and a swimming pool. The condominium complexes are also quite close to the beach.

Also of interest here, just to the south of Kepuhi Beach, separated from the latter by the Kaiak Rock, a 110-foot cinder cone, is the Papohaku Beach, one of Hawaii's largest white-sand beaches, some 3 miles long and, at places, nearly a hundred yards wide, bordered by *kiawe* trees. There are three access points to the beach: the first, off Kaluakoi Road, a mile or so south of the Kaluakoi Resort, leads to a developed beach park with showers and restrooms and some camping possibilities; the second, a little over a half-mile farther to the south, is by way of Lauhue Road, which goes off Kaluakoi Road; and the last, another three-quarters of a mile southward, is off Kalua

Road, which goes off Papapa Place, which, in turn, goes off Kaluakoi Road. The last two beach accesses, by the way, lead to essentially undeveloped beach parks, with the latter bordered by rocky outcroppings at its southern end, where, incidentally, Papohaku Beach finally ends.

There are, of course, other beaches along the coast here as well. South from Papohaku Beach, for instance, some 2 miles — reached on Kaluakoi Road and Poha Kuloa Road — lies the Kapukahehu Beach, popularly known as the "Dixie Maru Beach," named for the *Dixie Maru*, a sampan that wrecked just off the rocky coast here, in the 1920s. The beach, however, is small, crescent-shaped, and sandy, with good swimming possibilities.

Another beach here, north of the Kepuhi Beach — which fronts the Kaluakoi Resort — is the Pohaku Mauliuli Beach, a small, secluded, crescent-shaped white-sand beach, also known as Make Horse — or "Dead Horse" — Beach, named, evidently, for the fact that a horse once fell of a cliff here, and died. The beach, nevertheless, is an excellent place for picnicking, although swimming is not encouraged, due to the strong ocean currents, making it rather unsafe for the sport. The beach, of course, can be reached by way of Kaluakoi Road, some $4\frac{1}{2}$ miles from the Highway 450 intersection, then Kakaako Road northward — at the Paniolo Hale Condominiums — another quarter mile, and Leo Place west off Kakaaho Road, a half mile or so, directly to the beach.

Also try to visit the Kawakiu Beach, situated at the head of Kawakiu Nui Bay, a half mile or so north of Pohaku Mauliuli Beach (Make Horse Beach), and reached on Kaluakoi Road, northwest from Highway 450, then Kakaaho Road directly northward, until the paved portion of the road ends, from where a dirt trail leads another half mile, roughly, to the beach. Kawakiu Beach, interestingly, was the starting point for the celebrated Molokai-to-Oahu Canoe Race for several years, beginning in 1952, until the race was finally moved to the Hale O Lono harbor, along the southwest coast of the island, in 1963; and in 1975, it was also the scene of a peaceful demonstration by the Hui Alaloa, a group of Hawaiian activists, demanding public access to the beach, which was then granted by the Molokai Ranch Company. The beach, in any case, is one of Molokai's most beautiful beaches, sandy, secluded, and with excellent swimming possibilities during the summer months. It is also a good place for snorkeling, in calm seas, especially along the northern end of the cove, with its crystal clear waters and abundant coral.

Central Molokai

Central Molokai comprises primarily the vast dry plain connecting the island's two land masses, East Molokai and West Molokai. At the heart of it lies Hoolehua, a small town with only a post office — and with the Hoolehua Airport located just to the southwest of it — surrounded by 40-acre parcels of agricultural land, which were made available to native Hawaiians by the Hawaiian Homes Commission, beginning in 1932. Hoolehua, however, has one or two places of visitor interest quite close to it. Just to the east, for instance, about a mile from Highway 470 on Farrington Avenue, westward, then northwestward on Lihi Pali Avenue another half-mile or so, is Purdy's Macadamia Nut Farm, one of the island's foremost attractions, situated on a $1\frac{1}{2}$-acre Hawaiian homestead, and with a 60-year-old grove of some 45 macadamia nut trees. Here you can tour the orchard, and also learn all about the nuts — how they are grown, harvested, and processed, all naturally. Here, too, you can sample the nuts — both raw and roasted — as well as some delicious coconut and macadamia honey. Purdy's is open to the public Monday to Saturday, 9-1.

Also of interest, some $3\frac{1}{2}$ miles northwest of Hoolehua, reached on Farrington Avenue and Mo'omomi Road northwestward, and a short walk west along the shoreline, is Mo'omomi Beach, an essentially undeveloped stretch of beaches, bordering Mo'omomi Bay, and frequented primarily by fishermen. The Mo'omomi Beach area offers some beachcombing possibilities, although swimming and sunbathing are not recommended, due to the unsafe ocean conditions and strong afternoon tradewinds. However, some 2 miles to the west of Mo'omomi Bay, you can visit the island's only sand dunes, at a remote area known as Keonelele, or "flying sands, frequently also referred to as the "Desert Strip."

Yet another place of interest, situated just to the east of Hoolehua, at the intersection of Highways 470 and 480, is Kualapu'u, a small town with a plantation-era grid-style layout, and which has on its outskirts the world's largest rubber-lined reservoir — with a water capacity of 1.4 billion gallons! — built in the 1960s to supply water to central and west Molokai. In Kualapu'u itself, there is a market and restaurant, and a service station.

In any case, northwest from Kualapuu on Highway 470, some $2\frac{1}{2}$ miles, sits the village of Kalae, which has in it the R.W. Meyers Sugar Mill, an authentically restored mill, originally built in 1878 by Rudolf W. Meyers, a German immigrant who arrived in Molokai in 1850, married the high chieftainess, Kalama Waha, and had eleven children by her. Meyers managed the Molokai Ranch lands for King Kamehameha V, and also the Kalaupapa settlement just to the north, and successfully operated his sugar mill from 1878 until 1889. At the mill, of course, you can learn all about sugar production — from the crushing of the sugarcane to the heating, evaporating and cooling process, which produces a crystallized form of sugar and molasses, which is then placed in a centrifuge — powered by a steam engine — which separates the molasses from the final product — raw sugar. The mill museum also has several artifacts on display, centered, again, on sugar production. The mill is open to the public daily, 10 a.m.-12 noon.

North from the Meyers Sugar Mill, roughly a mile on Highway 470, lies the Palaau State Park, a splendid 234-acre park, at an elevation of approximately 1,600 feet, and which has in it forests of ironwood and eucalyptus, and good, abundant opportunities for picnicking and hiking. At the park, you can also visit the Kalaupapa Lookout, which has commanding views of the Kalaupapa Peninsula below, as well as interpretive displays, identifying and describing the various landmarks of the peninsula, among them the old lighthouse, built in 1909, at the northern tip of the peninsula, and the Kalaupapa settlement, the Kalaupapa Airfield, and the Kauhako Crater, along the southeast end of the peninsula. From here it is also easy to see how the 2,000-foot-high cliffs formed a natural barrier between Kalaupapa and the rest of Molokai. Near the park, too, are the Molokai Mule Ride stables, from where you can take a mule ride down to the Kalaupapa Peninsula, descending nearly 1,600 feet, zig-zagging along a narrow, 3-mile trail, with some 26 switchbacks.

Also at the Palaau State Park, a trail leads through groves of ironwood to Kaule O Nanahoa, or Phallic Rock, which, yes, resembles, in many ways, the male organ. Phallic Rock, of course, has its associations to a man named Nanahoa and his wife, Kawahuna, who, we are told, lived on this hill a long, long time ago. One day, however, according to legend, Nanahoa gazed and smiled upon a beautiful young girl who was looking at her reflection in a pool of water nearby. Kawahuna, quite understandably, became jealous, and grabbed the young girl by her hair. At which point, Nanahoa, outraged by his wife, struck her in anger and sent her tumbling down the hillside, where she turned to stone. But, as it turned out, Nanahoa, too, was turned to stone, but in the form of a phallus — hence the name, Phallic Rock. The rock, however, locals will tell you, is bestowed with magical powers of fertility, where childless women have spent the night and returned home, soon to conceive.

Kalaupapa

The Kalaupapa Peninsula is situated along the central part of Molokai's rugged north shore, surrounded on three sides by ocean, and on the fourth by 2,000-foot-high sea cliffs — some of the highest in the world. The peninsula, of course, was created by the Kauhako volcano, the crater of which can be seen at the southeast end of the peninsular tract.

The Kalaupapa Peninsula, tragically, is the site of Hawaii's infamous leper colony. Beginning in 1866, victims of the disease of leprosy were banished by the Hawaiian monarchy to this desolate corner of the island — a natural prison — frequently taken from their families and transported by ship to Kalawao, on the eastern side of the peninsula, where they were thrown overboard and left to fend for themselves. In 1873, however, Father Damien de Veuster, a Belgian priest, arrived at Kalaupapa, devoting himself to the care of the patients, who lived in great misery, without adequate food or shelter; but in 1884, he, too, contracted the disease, and five years later, in 1889, he died, at the age of 49. Father Damien's good work, nevertheless, was continued by Mother Marianne, who arrived at Kalaupapa in 1888, and lived and worked here tirelessly for the next

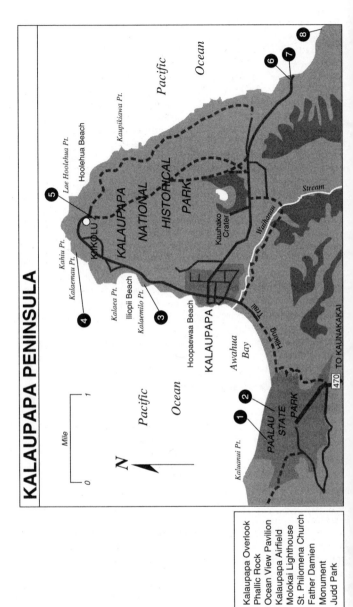

KALAUPAPA PENINSULA

Pacific Ocean

Kaupikiawa Pt.

Lae Hoolehua Pt.

Hoolehua Beach

KALAUPAPA NATIONAL HISTORICAL PARK

Kahiu Pt.

Kauhako Crater

Stream

Waikolu

Kalaemau Pt.

KUKOLU

Kalaea Pt.

Iliopii Beach

Kalaemilo Pt.

Hoopaewaa Beach

KALAUPAPA

Awahua Bay

Hiking Trail

Kalaunui Pt.

Pacific Ocean

PAALAU STATE PARK

470 TO KAUNAKAKAI

Mile

0   1

N

1. Kalaupapa Overlook
2. Phallic Rock
3. Ocean View Pavilion
4. Kalaupapa Airfield
5. Molokai Lighthouse
6. St. Philomena Church
7. Father Damien Monument
8. Judd Park

30 years, improving the health and living conditions of the patients at Kalaupapa, until her death at the age of 80. By the 1940s, of course, the discovery and introduction of sulfone drugs had rendered leprosy — or Hansen's Disease, as it had come to be known — a curable disease that was no longer contagious, and some years later, the inhabitants of Kalaupapa were cured and free to leave at their choosing. Most, however, chose to stay, for Kalaupapa was the only home they had known for much of their lives.

Kalaupapa is now a National Historical Park, where, however, the public is not permitted to wander unsupervised, for some 80 former patients still live there. Visitors, nevertheless, can take guided van tours of the settlement and the peninsula, taking in the Kalaupapa buildings, including a 1900s store and one or two dispensaries, and the white, steepled St. Philomena Church, built by Father Damien in 1872. On the tour you can also see other churches — Catholic, Protestant, Mormon — mostly dating from the 19th century, and visit the grassy Kalawao Park on the east side of the peninsula, overlooking the ocean and the north coast of the island, as well as the Kalaupapa museum-cum-bookstore, which has old photos recounting the history of Kalaupapa and its inhabitants, and books on Father Damien, Mother Marianne, and Kalaupapa.

Kalaupapa, by the way, can be reached on foot, by hiking down from the Palaau State Park, some 1,600 feet, which takes approximately an hour, and one and one-half hours back up; or on a scheduled flight directly to the Kalaupapa Airfield.

Waikolu Lookout and Kamakou Preserve

There remains yet another area to explore on Molokai. Northwestward from Kaunakakai on Highway 460, some 4 miles, the rugged Maunahui Road — the main forest road — dashes off into the wild, mountainous terrain to the east, climbing more than 3,000 feet, to the Waikolu Lookout, and passing by, some 9 miles from the highway turnoff, Lua Na Moku 'Iliahi — the Sandalwood Measuring Pit — where you can still see the eroded pit in the clearing, originally dug out in the 1800s to duplicate, in shape and size, a ship's hold. The pit, of course, was used as a measure during the days of the sandalwood trade. Typically, the sandalwood pit would be filled with sandalwood logs, representing a ship load, and at the end of negotiations between the island's chiefs and the ships' captains, the sandalwood would be transferred to the ships waiting just off shore

In any case, a mile or so past the Sandalwood Measuring Pit is the Wailoku Lookout, at an elevation of 3,700 feet, from where you can see the lush, amphitheater-like Wailoku Valley, frequently rain-soaked and dotted with waterfalls and streams. From the Wailoku Valley, interestingly, a $5\frac{1}{2}$-mile water tunnel, bored through the valley itself, channels rainwater into the Kualapuu Reservoir, at Kualapuu. At the Wailoku Lookout, too, there is a grassy picnic area, as well as some camping possibilities.

Finally, just to the east of the Wailoku Lookout lies the expansive, 2,774-acre Kamakou Preserve, which has in it, more or less at its center, the lofty Mt. Kamakou, the highest peak on Molokai, at an elevation of 4,970 feet. The Kamakou Preserve, of course, originally established in 1982 by the Nature Conservancy of Hawaii, is a nature wonderland of sorts, filled with rain forests and lush, rain-soaked valleys, and home to no fewer than five endangered species of birds, including two that are found only on Molokai, the Molokai Creeper and Molokai Thrush. There are several species of native Hawaiian plants and ferns here as well, and also some groves of rare Hawaiian sandalwood trees. Besides which, the area has a fair number of hiking trails, meandering, quite enchantingly, through the lush wilderness. It is, however, a good idea, we might suggest, to contact the Nature Conservancy of Hawaii, at (808) 553-5236, for current information on the trails, before striking out on foot into the misty wilderness.

PRACTICAL INFORMATION FOR MOLOKAI

HOW TO GET THERE

Molokai lies roughly $8\frac{1}{2}$ miles northwest of Maui, with Lanai directly to its south, some 9 miles, and with Oahu 25 miles to the northwest. It can be reached from the U.S. mainland by way of Maui, either on a scheduled commercial flight or by ferry boat; or by way of Honolulu, Oahu, which is serviced by several different domestic as well as international airlines. Commercial flights to and from Molokai arrive and depart at the island's main airport, the *Molokai Airport*, located at Hoolehua, in central Molokai; while ferries ply between Lahaina, Maui, and Molokai's *Kaunakakai Harbor*. There is also a small commuter airfield, the *Kalaupapa Airfield*, located on the Kalaupapa Peninsula, on the island's north shore.

By Air

Direct flights to Molokai from Kahului, Maui, and Honolulu, Oahu, are available on the following airlines: *Air Molokai* (808) 877-0026; *Aloha Airlines* (808) 244-9071; *Aloha IslandAir* (800) 652-6541; and *Hawaiian Airlines* (800) 882-8811. For schedules and fare information, contact the respective airlines. (For flights from the U.S. mainland to Maui and Honolulu, Oahu, see *How To Get There* in the *Maui* section.)

By Ferry

Ferry services are available daily between Kaunakakai, Molokai, and Lahaina, Maui, on board the *Maui Princess*. One-way adult fare is $25.00. For departure and arrival times and more information, contact *Maui Princess*, 505 Front St., Room 225, Lahaina; (808) 661-8397/(800) 833-5800.

TOURIST INFORMATION

Hawaii Visitors Bureau (HVB). Waikiki Business Plaza, 2270 Kalakaua Ave., Suite 808, Honolulu, HI 96815. Offers a wealth of tourist information, including directory of accommodations and restaurants and a calendar of events. Also maps, and a tourist publication, *The Islands of Hawaii: A Vacation Planner*, covering places of interest on the islands, recreation and tours. The Hawaii Visitors Bureau also maintains an office on Maui, for visitors arriving in Molokai from Maui; *Maui Visitors Bureau,* 250 Alamaha St., Kahului, HI 96733; (808) 871-8691.

Destination Molokai Association. P.O. Box 960, Kaunakakai, HI 96748; (808) 553-3876/(800) 367-ISLE. Also offers visitor information, for accommodations, restaurants, tours and events on Molokai.

Maui County Department of Parks and Recreation (Molokai Office). P.O. Box 526, Kaunakakai, HI 96748; (808) 553-3204. Information and permits for camping in county park areas in Molokai.

HOW TO GET AROUND

By Car. Rental cars are available from a half-dozen or so different car rental agencies on the island, most of them located at the Molokai Airport in Hoolehua. Rental rates for sub-compacts to larger luxury cars range from $18-$70 per day to $180-$320 per week. Most of the companies also offer four-wheel-drive vehicles, especially useful if you plan to visit some of the more remote parts of the island. For rentals, availability and more information, contact any of the following: *Avis* (800) 831-8000, *Budget* (808) 244-4721, *Dollar* (800) 342-7398/(808) 567-6156, *Sunshine Rent A Car* (808) 567-6118, or *USA Rent A Car* (808) 567-6118.

By Taxi. The following taxi companies service the island: *Friendly Isle Tours & Transportation,* (808) 567-6177; *Kukui Tours & Limo,* (808) 553-5133; *Molokai Off-Road Tours & Taxi,* (808) 553-3369; and *T.E.E.M. Cab Molokai,* (808) 553-3433. For fares and service areas, contact the respective companies.

ACCOMMODATIONS

Colony's Kaluakoi Hotel & Golf Club. *$90-$200.* Kaluakoi Rd. (off Hwy. 460), Maunaloa; (808) 552-2555/(800) 777-1700. Oceanfront resort hotel, with 177 rooms and suites. TV, phones, some kitchens; also swimming pool, tennis courts, golf course, restaurant and cocktail lounge, and meeting rooms on premises.

Paniolo Hale. *$95-$160.* Kaluakoi Rd. (off Hwy.460), Maunaloa; (808) 552-2731/(800) 367-2984. 39 condominium units, with TV, phones, ceiling fans, and kitchens; also private lanais with hot tubs. Swimming pool, and paddle court. Weekly maid service. Minimum stay: 3 nights.

Hotel Molokai. *$55-$100.* Kamehameha V Hwy. (450), Kaunakakai; (808) 553-5347/(800) 423-MOLO. 55 oceanfront condominium units; private baths, and lanais. Swimming pool and restaurant and cocktail lounge on premises.

Kaluakoi Villas. *$45-$75.* Kephui Beach, Maunaloa; (808) 552-2721/(800) 225-7978/(800) 525-1470. 300-unit beachfront condominium complex with studios and 1-bedroom units. TV, phones; swimming, restaurant and cocktail lounge.

Ke Nani Kai. *$105-$150.* Maunaloa; (808) 552-2761/(800) 888-2791. 120 one- and two-bedroom condominium units in West Molokai, with TV and phones; some ocean views. Also swimming pool, and tennis courts.

Molokai Shores. *$85-$125.* Kamehameha V Hwy.(450), Kaunakakai; (808) 553-5954/(800) 535-0085. 42 1- and 2-bedroom units in oceanfront condominium complex. TV, and kitchens. Also swimming pool, putting green and barbeque area.

Pau Hana Inn. *$45-$90.* Oki St., Kaunakakai; (808) 553-5342/(800) 423-MOLO. Beachfront hotel with 40 units. Swimming pool, restaurant and cocktail lounge. Live entertainment on Fridays and Saturdays.

Wavecrest Resort. *$60-$90.* Star Route 155, Kaunakakai; (808) 558-8103. Oceanfront condominium complex, with 21 units with TV and kitchens, located 13 miles east of Kaunakakai. Swimming pool and tennis courts on premises. Minimum stay, 3 nights.

SEASONAL EVENTS

January

Fourth Weekend. *Ka Molokai Makahiki.* Held at the Kaunakakai Baseball Field in Kaunakakai. Ancient Hawaiian holiday, devoted to sports, games and celebration of life. Variety of music, food, and traditional Hawaiian games, including spear throwing and Hawaiian wrestling. For a schedule of events, call (808) 553-3876.

March

Fourth Weekend. *Prince Kuhio Day.* Celebration honoring Prince Kuhio, Hawaii's first delegate to the U.S. Congress; held in Kaunakakai.

Features entertainment, and food concessions. For more information, call Destination Molokai at (808) 553-3876.

April

First Weekend. *Buddha Day.* Celebration of the birth of Buddha, with Buddhist festivities, including flower pageants, staged at Buddhist temples throughout the islands. For more information, call (808) 536-7044.

May

Third Weekend. *Molokai Ka Hula Piko.* At the Papohaku Beach in Kaluakoi. Celebration of the birth of the hula, drawing a crowd of approximately 2,000 people. Features traditional Hawaiian arts and crafts, music, and local foods. For more information, call Destination Molokai at (808) 553-3876 or (800) 800-6367 in Oahu. *Bankoh Kayak Challenge.* 38-mile kayak race, beginning at Laau Point, at Colony's Kaluakoi Hotel & Golf Club in Molokai, and ending at the Koko Marina, at Hawaii Kai, on Oahu. (808) 254-5055.

July

First Weekend. *4th of July.* Independence day parade held in Kaunakakai, and fireworks display at Oneali'i Beach Park, 3 miles east of Kaunakakai.

September

Fourth Weekend. *Bankoh Na Wahine o Ke Kai.* Women's 40.8-mile Molokai-to-Oahu outrigger canoe race, beginning at Hale o Lono Harbor in Molokai, and finishing at Duke Kahanamoku Beach, Waikiki. For more information, call (808) 262-7567. *Molokai Music Festival.* Held at the Meyer Sugar Mill in Kalae. Features live music, presented by local Molokai performers; also hula dancing and demonstrations of traditional arts and crafts, and food concessions. For more information, call (808) 567-6436/(800) 553-0404.

October

First Week. *Aloha Week.* Week-long festival, with events staged throughout the island. Features a variety of Hawaiian pageantry and demonstrations in lei making, poi pounding, coconut husking and coconut weaving. Also parades, arts and crafts, food, island fruit tasting, and entertainment — including original Hawaiian music and hula dancers. For a schedule of events, locations, and more information, call (808) 944-8857.

Second Weekend. *Bankoh Molokai Hoe.* Men's 40.8-mile Molokai-to-Oahu outrigger canoe race, beginning at Hale o Lono Harbor in Molokai, and finishing at Fort DeRussy Beach in Waikiki. (808) 261-6614.

December

First Weekend. *Bodhi Day.* Traditional Buddhist celebrations at temples throughout the islands, marking the Buddhist Day of Enlightenment. For more information, call (808) 536-7044.

PLACES OF INTEREST

Big Wind Kite Factory. 120 Maunaloa Hwy., Maunaloa; (808) 552-2364. Unique specialty store, offering an assortment of colorful, handcrafted kites; also kite flying lessons, and factory tours. Open daily.

Purdy's Natural Macadamia Nut Farm. Located Lihi Pali Ave. (which goes off Farrington Ave., which, in turn, goes off Hwy. 470), in Hoolehua; (808) 567-6601/(808) 567-6495. This is one of Molokai's foremost attractions, situated on a 1½-acre Hawaiian homestead, with a 60-year-old grove of some 45 macadamia nut trees. Offers a tour of the orchard, explaining all about the nuts — how they are grown, harvested and processed, all naturally. Also sampling of nuts, both raw and roasted, as well as delicious coconut and macadamia honey. Open Mon.-Sat., 9 a.m.-2 p.m. Free admission.

R. W. Meyer Sugar Mill. Located on Hwy. 470, 4 miles north of intersection of Hwy. 460, in Kalae; (808) 567-6436. Authentically restored sugar mill, originally built in 1878. Now a museum and cultural center, featuring several artifacts of interest, centered around the sugar industry. Also exhibits and tour describing the entire sugar-making process. Open 10-12 daily. Admission: $2.50.

Ili'iliopae Heiau. Located off Kamehameha V Hwy. (450), approximately 15½ miles of Kaunakakai; reached by way of a dirt road which goes north off the highway, a ½ mile past mile marker 15, then onto the Wailau Trail which leads directly to the *heiau*. The *heiau* is on private property; permission to visit the *heiau* may be obtained from *Destination Molokai Association*, (808) 553-3876, or *Molokai Trail and Wagon Ride*, (808) 558-8380. The Ili'iliopae Heiau is Molokai's oldest and largest *heiau*, with an 87-foot-wide and 286-foot-long platform, which is originally believed to have been 920 feet long. In ancient times, the *heiau* was both a place of worship and human sacrifice.

Kalaupapa Peninsula. Situated on Molokai's remote north shore, beneath 2,000-foot cliffs, and reached by way of a steep, narrow 3-mile hiking trail with 26 switchbacks, or by air. The peninsula itself, isolated from the rest of the island, was once the site of a leper colony, established in 1866, and finally abandoned in the 1940s. It is now preserved as the *Kalaupapa National Historical Park*, with tours of the area available to visitors. Tours take in the Kalaupapa settlement and its buildings, including a 1900s store, one or two dispensaries, the white, steepled St. Philomena Church, built by Father Damien in 1872, and the 19th-century Catholic, Protestant and Mormon churches. Also included on the tour are a visit to the Kalawao Park, on the east side of the peninsula, and the Kalaupapa museum-cum-bookstore, which has old photos recounting the history of Kalaupapa and its inhabitants, as well as books on Father Damien, Mother Marianne, and Kalaupapa. For touring information and visitor permits (which are required to visit the peninsula), contact *Father Damien Tours* at (808) 567-6171.

Upper Moa'ula Falls, cascading over 250 feet, in the Halawa Valley, Molokai

Pali (cliffs) above the Kalaupapa Peninsula in Molokai

Halawa Valley. Located at the east end of the island, approximately 27 miles from Kaunakakai, reached more or less directly on Kamehameha V Hwy. (450). Lush, green valley, site of the first recorded settlement on Molokai, dating from 650 A.D. The valley has in it, as its chief attractions, the *Halawa Beach Park*, situated along Halawa Bay, at the mouth of the Halawa River; and the *Moa'ula* and *Hipuapua* waterfalls, 250 feet and 500 feet, respectively, located farther upriver. The Moa'ula Falls can be reached by way of a rugged, $2\frac{1}{2}$-mile hiking trail that goes off the highway (450), roughly a quarter mile south of the Halawa Beach Park; and the Hipuapua Falls Trail branches off the Moa'ula Falls trail, just before reaching the Moa'ula Falls. There is also a rather difficult trail leading to the Upper Moa'ula Falls, which, too, branches off the Moa'ula Falls trail, a hundred yards or so before reaching the latter.

Palaau State Park. At the end of Kalae Hwy. (470), approximately a mile north of Kalae (or $3\frac{1}{2}$ miles northeast of Hoolehua). 234-acre state park, at an elevation of 1,600 feet, overlooking the Kalaupapa Peninsula. Good picnicking and hiking possibilities, with trails leading through groves of ironwood and eucalyptus, to the Kalaupapa Lookout and the legendary Phallic Rock. The park is open to the public daily.

Molokai Ranch Wildlife Park. Off Kaluakoi Rd. (which goes off Hwy. 460), Maunaloa; (808) 552-2741. 1,000-acre, African safari-type wild animal park, where more than 800 exotic animals, mainly African and Asian, roam freely — including giraffes, barbary sheep, greater kudu, oryx, sable antelope, rhea, eland and zebra — which can be seen on guided, $1\frac{1}{2}$-hour van tours of the park. Tours depart from the nearby Kaluakoi Resort. Call for tour schedule and reservations.

Kamakou Preserve. Northeast of Kaunakakai, approximately 8 miles; reached by way of Hwy. 460 northwestward some 4 miles, then the mountainous Maunahui Rd. directly east another 8 miles to the reserve. Large, 2,774-acre preserve, which has in it Mt. Kamakou, the highest peak on the island, at an elevation of 4,970 feet. The park itself is a nature wonderland of sorts, filled with rain-forests and lush valleys, and home to at least five endangered species of birds, including the Molokai Creeper and Molokai Thrush. The park also has in it several species of native Hawaiian plants and ferns, and some groves of rare Hawaiian sandalwood trees. Good hiking possibilities; for wilderness trail information, contact the Nature Conservancy of Hawaii, at (808) 553-5236.

BEACHES

Oneali'i Beach Park. Located 3 miles east of Kaunakakai, off Kamehameha V Hwy. (450). Narrow, sandy beach, with shallow water, ideal for swimming for children. Facilities include a pavilion, restrooms and ballpark. There is also an ancient fishpond at the beach.

Murphey's Beach Park. Off Kamehameha V Hwy. (450), 20 miles east of Kaunakakai. Sandy beach, protected by a reef just offshore, offering safe swimming conditions for children. Views of Moku Ho'oniki Island and Kanaha Rock to the northeast. No beach facilities.

Halawa Beach Park. At the end of Kamehameha V Hwy. (450), approximately 27 miles east of Kaunakakai. The beach park is situated inside along Halawa Bay, and is generally safe for swimming, except during high seas. Popular with surfers, and fishermen. Facilities include a pavilion, barbecue grills, and restrooms.

Kepuhi Beach. Situated off Kaika Rd., which goes off Kaluakoi Rd., at the Kaluakoi Resort. Long, sandy beach, fronting on the Kaluakoi Hotel. Offers spectacular sunsets, and view of the island of Oahu, some 25 miles to the northwest. Good sunbathing possibilities; swimming not advised, due to dangerous ocean conditions. No beach facilities.

Papohaku Beach. Situated just south of Kepuhi Beach and the Kaluakoi Resort, off Kaluakoi Rd., with at least three different access roads leading down to the beach. This is one of Hawaii's largest and most beautiful white-sand beaches, 3 miles long and, at places, nearly a hundred yards wide, bordered by kiawe trees. Views of Oahu; and showers and restroom facilities at one of the beach access points. Swimming not advised, due to the strong under-currents.

Kapukahehu Beach (Dixie Maru Beach). Located 2 miles south of Papohaku Beach, at the end of Poha Kuloa Rd., which goes off Kaluakoi Rd., at its southwestern end. Small, crescent-shaped sandy beach. Offers safe swimming conditions, except during high surf.

Pohaku Mauliuli Beach (Make Horse Beach). North of Kepuhi Beach and the Kaluakoi Resort; reached by way of Kakaako Rd. (which goes off Kaluakoi Rd. at the Paniolo Hale Condominiums), then westward on Leo Place to the end. Picturesque, crescent-shaped beach, which, however, is unsafe for swimming due to the prevailing ocean conditions here. No facilities.

Kawakiu Beach. Situated on Kawakiu Nui Bay, north of the Kaluakoi Hotel; reached by way of a dirt trail that goes off Kakaako Rd. (which goes off Kaluakoi Rd.), at the very end, near the 14th green of Kaluakoi Golf Course, passing through arid stretches overgrown with kiawe trees. Lovely, secluded beach, crescent-shaped and sandy. Swimming not advised during the winter and spring months.

Mo'omomi Beach. Located approximately 3½ miles northwest of hoolehua, bordering Mo'omomi Bay; reached by way of Farrington Ave., which turns into a rutted, dirt road, to the very end. Long, undeveloped beach, frequented primarily by fishermen. Beachcombing possibilities; unsafe for swimming due to the prevailing ocean conditions and strong afternoon winds. No facilities.

GOLF COURSES

Ironwood Hills Golf Club. Kualapuu; (808) 567-6000. 9-hole par-34 course, with good views of the island. Green fees: $10.00; with cart rental, $17.00; additional rounds, $5.00. Club rentals available.

Kaluakoi Golf Club. At the Kaluakoi Resort, Kaluakoi Rd., Maunaloa; (808) 552-2739. 18-hole, par-72, oceanfront course. Green fees: $75.00 (including cart). Pro shop, driving range and putting green; also club rentals.

TOURS

Friendly Isle Tours & Transportation. Kaunakakai; (808) 553-9046. Offers full-day and half-day scenic tours of the island. Tour cost: $20.00-$50.00 per person.

Kukui Tours & Limousine. 855 Palapalai Pl., Kaunakakai; (808) 553-5133. Half-day and full-day sightseeing tours of west and central Molokai; also tours of east Molokai. Cost of tours: Half-day, $20.00; full-day, $37.00.

Molokai Charters. P.O. Box 1207, Kaunakakai, HI 96748; (808) 553-5852. Sailing charters of varying lengths, from 2 hours to half-day and full-day. The full-day trips include snorkeling and lunch at Lanai. Cost: 2-hour tour, $35.00; Half-day tour, $50.00; and full-day tour, $85.00.

Father Damien Tours. Kalaupapa; (808) 567-6171. Offers guided van tours of the Kalaupapa Peninsula, with pick-up points at the bottom of the Pali trail and at the Kalaupapa Airport. Tours include all the points of interest on Kalaupapa, including the historic St. Philomena Church, built by Father Damien in 1872, and the Kalaupapa museum-cum-bookstore, which has old, historic photos on display, as well as a good selection of books on Kalaupapa. Tour cost: $25.00 per person (must be 16 years of age or older). Advance reservations and permits required.

Molokai Ranch Wildlife Park. Maunaloa; (808) 552-2741/552-2555. Guided, 1½-hour van tours of 1,000-acre, African safari-type wild animal park, where more than 800 exotic wild animals can be seen, including giraffes, barbary sheep, greater kudu, oryx, sable antelope, rhea, eland and zebra. Tours depart from the Kaluakoi Resort at Maunaloa; reservations advisable. Tour cost: $35.00 adults, $25.00 children 5-12, $10.00 under 5.

Molokai Trail and Wagon Ride. P.O. Box 56, Hoolehua, HI 96729; (808) 558-8380. Tour of Mapulehu Valley, as well as mango orchards and the ancient Ili'iliopae Heiau. Tours depart at 10.30 a.m. daily (except Sundays), and include lunch at Hotel Molokai in Kaunakakai. Cost of tours: $29.00-$40.00 per person.

Fishing Charters. The following fishing boats are available for full-day and half-day charters: *Shon-A-Lei II,* (808) 553-5242; and *The Alyce C,* (808) 558-8377. Rates range from $225.00 for half-day trips to $425.00 for full-day charters.

RESTAURANTS

(Restaurant prices — based on full-course dinner, excluding drinks, tax and tips — are categorized as follows: *Deluxe,* over $30; *Expensive,* $20-$30; *Moderate,* $10-$20; *Inexpensive,* under $10.)

Holoholo Kai. *Moderate.* At the Hotel Molokai, Kamehameha V Hwy. (450), Kaunakakai; (808) 553-5347. Open-air setting; overlooking the ocean and with views of the island of Lanai. Fresh local seafood, steaks and poultry dishes; also salad bar. Entertainment. Open for breakfast, lunch and dinner.

Jojo's Cafe. *Inexpensive.* Maunaloa Hwy. (460), Maunaloa; (808) 552-2803. Specialties here are fish and burgers, and a hearty Portuguese bean soup. Open for lunch and dinner (closed Wed. and Sun.).

Kanemitsu Bakery & Restaurant. *Inexpensive.* Ala Malama, Kaunakakai; (808) 553-5855. Famous for its freshly-baked "Molokai Bread." Also burgers and plate lunches. Open for breakfast, lunch and dinner.

Kualapuu Cook House. *Inexpensive.* Kualapuu; (808) 567-6185. Fresh fish, chicken and beef, served with a variety of sauces, with rice. Also burgers, chili, and a variety of pies. Open for breakfast, lunch and dinner, Mon.-Sat.

Molokai Drive Inn. *Inexpensive.* Kaunakakai; (808) 553-5655. Hamburgers, hot dogs, chili and salads; also chicken stew, shrimp, fried saimin, and ice cream. Plate lunches. Open for breakfast, lunch and dinner daily.

Ohia Lodge Restaurant. *Moderate.* At Colony's Kaluakoi Hotel & Golf Club, Kaluakoi Rd., Maunaloa; (808) 552-2555. Spectacular sunsets, and views of Oahu. Serves primarily Continental cuisine, including prime rib and fresh seafood. Entertainment and dancing. Open for breakfast, lunch and dinner. Reservations suggested.

Outpost Natural Foods. *Inexpensive.* Kaunakakai; (808) 553-3377. Offers a variety of natural foods, including sandwiches, burritos and fruit smoothies. Open for lunch, Mon.-Sat.

Oviedo's Lunch Counter. *Inexpensive.* Puali Rd., Kaunakakai; (808) 553-5014. Home-style Filipino food. House specialty is pork adobo. Lunch daily.

Pau Hana Inn. *Inexpensive-Moderate.* Seaside Pl., Kaunakakai; (808) 553-5342. Fresh seafood, beef and poultry dishes. Open for breakfast, lunch and dinner.

LANAI

"The Private Isle"

Lanai is Hawaii's "Private Isle," set in splendid isolation. It was, until recently, also famous as Hawaii's "Pineapple Island," with more than 16,000 acres once planted to the fruit, comprising the world's largest pineapple plantation. Pineapple, however, has now largely given way to tourism as the island's principal industry. The island's first resorts, the Lodge at Koele and the Manele Bay Hotel, opened in 1991 and 1992, respectively, as did two new, championship golf courses and several new shops, to add to Lanai's visitor facilities. The island, nevertheless, has retained, for the most part, its simple charm, much of it still wild and unspoilt, with only 30 miles of paved roads, all told, and with remote beaches all along its uninhabited north coast, ruins of ancient fishing villages on its east coast, the eerie landscape of the "Garden of the Gods" in its northwest, and pastoral Palawai Basin and the lofty, 3,370-foot Lanaihale ridge more or less at its center. It remains, thus, an island of back roads, ideally suited to the outdoor enthusiast, and best explored in a four-wheel-drive vehicle or, often enough, on foot.

Lanai is the sixth largest — or third smallest — of the main Hawaiian islands, some 18 miles long and 13 miles wide, encompassing roughly 140 square miles. At its center sits Lanai City, the island's only town; at its south lie the beautiful Manele and Hulopoe bays, the most popular coastal strip; along the north and east coast, respectively, are the Shipwreck and Keomuku beaches, made up of several smaller pockets of sand; and at the northwest end of the island lies the strange, natural phenomenon of the "Garden of the Gods." Yet another tour takes in the lush, Norfolk pine-lined Munro Trail, just to the east of Lanai City, which journeys over the Lanaihale ridge, the island's highest point.

Lanai is situated approximately equidistant — 9 miles — from Maui and Molokai, which lie to its east and north, respectively. The island can be reached by ferry from Maui, or on inter-island flights from Maui, Molokai or Oahu. The island's main airport, the Lanai Airport, is located near the southwest end of the island, some 3 miles from Lanai City.

LANAI

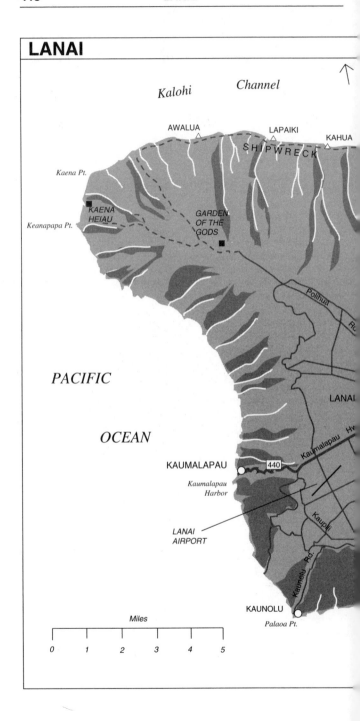

Kalohi Channel

AWALUA

LAPAIKI

KAHUA

SHIPWRECK

Kaena Pt.

KAENA HEIAU

Keanapapa Pt.

GARDEN OF THE GODS

Polihua Rd.

PACIFIC

OCEAN

LANAI

Kaumalapau Hwy

KAUMALAPAU

440

Kaumalapau Harbor

Kaupili

LANAI AIRPORT

Kaunolu Rd.

KAUNOLU

Palaoa Pt.

Miles

0   1   2   3   4   5

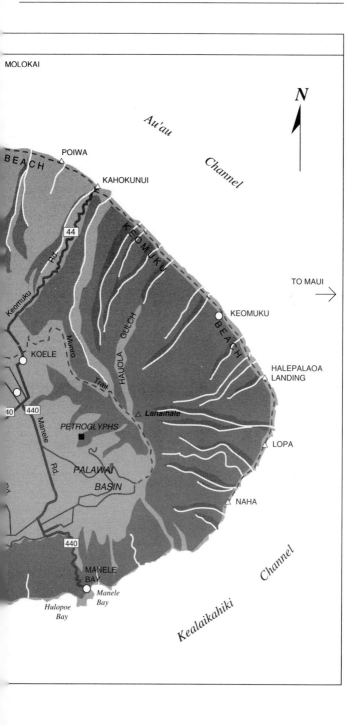

DISCOVERING LANAI

Lanai City

Lanai City is Lanai's chief population center, and its only town, as such, situated more or less at the center of the island, to the north of Palawai Basin, at an elevation of 1,624 feet. It was originally built in the early 1920s as a plantation town, by James Dole's Hawaii Pineapple Company which, in 1922, also purchased the island — yes, the entire island! — for a reported $1.1 million. The town is now home to a majority of the island's approximately 2,200 inhabitants, and quite picturesque, filled with the characteristic Norfolk Island pines and old, tin-roofed plantation-era houses, mostly set along a grid of a dozen or so paved streets.

Lanai City itself is one mile long and a half mile wide, and it has at the center of it the grassy, Norfolk pine-lined Dole Park, with most of the local businesses — a shopping center, a market, two eateries, and a handful of shops — situated around the park, on Seventh, Eighth, Fraser and Lanai avenues. Here, too, at the southwest corner of Dole Park, is the town's jail, comprising three adjoining, free-standing cells, situated directly in front of the police station; and near the southeast end of the park, on Lanai Avenue, stands the venerable old Hotel Lanai, originally built in the 1920s to accommodate James Dole's guests and visiting company executives. The hotel, for nearly seven decades, offered the only visitor accommodations on the island, with 10 guest rooms and a restaurant-cum-bar to boot. It remains quite popular with locals and visitors alike, most of them gathering here to exchange local gossip; and, needless to say, it continues to offer overnight lodging to guests.

One of the newest additions to Lanai City, of course, is the elegant Lodge at Koele, situated along Highway 44, just to the northeast of town, and nestled amid green meadows and towering pines, and well-kept gardens overflowing with halaconias, orchids and torch ginger. The lodge opened to the public only recently, in 1991, and it offers in it 102 well-appointed guest rooms, restaurants, swimming pool, tennis courts, lawn bowling and croquet facilities, and an 18-hole, Greg Norman and Ted Robinson-designed, championship golf course. The lodge also has a notable art collection, of European and Pacific paintings and sculpture.

Also of interest, some 6 miles southwest of Lanai City, at the end of the Kaumalapau Highway (440), is the Kaumalapau Harbor, also built by the Dole interests, to ship the company's pineapple to its canneries in Honolulu, and from where more than a million pineapples are now shipped daily. Here, too, as you approach the Kaumalapau Harbor, you can see, toward the north, five sea stacks, variously known as Nanahoa, Three Stones, and The Needles. The harbor, besides, is also a good place to enjoy Lanai's beautiful sunsets.

LANAI CITY

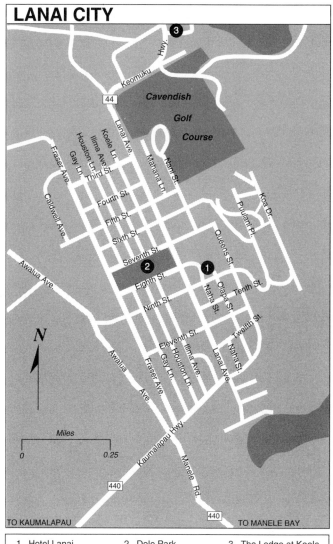

1. Hotel Lanai   2. Dole Park   3. The Lodge at Koele

Manele Bay and Hulopoe Bay

Directly south from Lanai City, some 7 miles on the Manele Road — or Highway 440 south — lies Manele Bay, a popular little boat harbor, open to private as well as commercial boats, and which, before James Dole purchased the island in 1922, was used by Lanai's previous owner, the Lanai Ranch Company, to ship cattle. The remnants of a cattle ramp can still be seen along the west side of the harbor. Nearby, also, are the ruins of an ancient fishing village, with some foundations of some old Hawaiian houses still visible.

Also of interest, a little to the southwest of Manele Bay is Pu'u Pehe Cove, with a small, sandy beach, and just offshore from there rises a sea stack, the Pu'u Pehe Rock, also known as Sweetheart Rock, site of a tragic tale. Legend endures that Pu'u Pehe, a beautiful Mauian woman, was kidnapped by a young warrior from Lanai, who, afraid that she would leave him, hid her in a sea cave here. But one day, while he was away, fetching fresh water, a kona storm suddenly descended upon the area, sending huge waves of water gushing into the cave, trapping and killing the woman. The young warrior, upon discovering the tragedy, became distraught, and carried Pu'u Pehe to the top of Sweetheart Rock, where he built a tomb for her; and not long after, he took his own life, jumping off the rock into the crashing sea below.

In any event, adjoining to the west of Pu'u Pehe Cove is Hulopoe Bay, at the head of which lies the crescent-shaped white-sand Hulopoe Beach, one of Hawaii's loveliest beaches, which, besides good swimming possibilities, offers some of the best snorkeling in the islands, with its abundant marine life and coral, all protected as part of the Manele-Hulopoe Marine Life Conservatory District. The beach also has picnic tables and barbecue pits, volleyball courts, and a nearby wading pool for children, blasted from rock in 1951.

Directly above Hulopoe Beach, of course, situated on a bluff overlooking both the beach and nearby Manele Bay, is the newly-built, luxury Manele Bay Hotel, developed in only 1991. The hotel offers 250 oceanview rooms, two plush restaurants — including one that features koa wood furnishings and decor, in the traditional Hawaiian monarch style — a large swimming pool overlooking the beach, tennis courts, and an 18-hole golf course designed by Jack Nicklaus. The hotel also has some splendid gardens, Japanese, Hawaiian and Filipino, and a collection of South Pacific art.

Kaunolu

Kaunolu, situated at the southwest corner of the island, some 7 or 8 miles from Lanai City, is the site of an ancient fishing village, which once was also the favorite vacation retreat of Kamehameha I, and where you can still see the sites of some 86 houses and 35 shelters — one of the best preserved ruins in the Hawaiian islands. However, getting to Kaunolu, to say the least, can be an experience in itself, journeying through pineapple fields and down rutted, dusty trails, largely unmarked. Nevertheless, for the stout of heart and limb, we suggest following Manele Road — Highway 440 — south from Lanai City, nearly 4 miles, until the road makes a sharp left; here, rather than follow the highway to the left, continue straight ahead, onto a dirt road — which has a sign pointing to Kaunolu, and which, incidentally, is the Kaupili Road — passing through pineapple fields. From the intersection of Kaupili Road and the highway (440), it is roughly 2½ miles to the fourth dirt road on the left — which, by the way, is the Kaunolu Road, although you may not know this! — and which dashes off toward the ocean, another 3 miles or so — making a sharp left just three quarters of a mile from the turnoff and a sharp right a quarter mile farther — along an especially bumpy descent, to Kaunolu.

In any event, at the end of Kaunolu Road — which goes to the right at the three-way intersection, at the very bottom, at Kaunolu — you can search out the site of Kamehameha I's summer home, where you can still see the platform. Also, westward from here, across a gulch, you can see a large, domineering structure, the Halulu Heiau, reached by way of a short walk down the embankment and across the gulch to some stone walls on the opposite bank, from where a trail leads more or less directly to the *heiau*. There are also some petroglyphs here, depicting humans, birds and dancers, located just to the west of the *heiau*.

Westward from the Halulu Heiau and the petroglyphs, too, atop the sea cliffs, is the legendary Kahekili's Leap, a sheer, 90-foot drop to the crystal clear waters below, and from where, we are told, King Kamehameha I would force his warriors to jump, as a test of their courage and worthiness. Near to Kahekili's Leap, and also of interest, is the Kolokolo Cave, in which you can hear the waves crashing and thundering; and just off shore from here is Moku Naio, or Shark Island, with its surprising resemblance to the fin of a shark. There are, by the way, good scuba diving and snorkeling possibilities here as well.

Finally, in Kaunolu itself you can search out the ancient house sites, well over a hundred, mostly scattered through the Kaunolu Gulch, and where, it is estimated, some 400 to 500 people may have once lived.

The Munro Trail

A highlight of any visit to Lanai, it must be fair to say, is a drive — or hike — up the Munro Trail, an 8-mile trail, just to the east of Lanai City, that winds through groves of Norfolk Island pine and a lush, tropical rain forest, journeying over the Lanaihale ridge — the highest point in Lanai, at an elevation of 3,370 feet. The trail, of course, is named for George C. Munro, an environmentalist and a native of New Zealand, who, while manager of the Lanai Ranch Company in the early 1900s, began planting seeds of the Norfolk

Island Pine, indigenous to New Zealand, throughout the island, to increase the island's water-drawing capacities. The Norfolk pine, needless to say, is now characteristic of the island, abundant throughout Lanai City and along the Munro Trail.

In any case, the trailhead can be reached by following Keomuku Road — Highway 44 — north from Lanai City, approximately 2 miles, then off on a paved road that goes off to the right — eastward — passing by a cemetery, another half mile or so, at which point it becomes a dirt trail — the Munro Trail. From here, you can follow the signs for the Munro Trail, winding through groves of pine, eucalyptus and ironwood, as well as a lush, tropical rain forest, and with spectacular views of the Maunalei and Wahane gulches, to the northeast.

Of interest, too, some 2½ miles along the trail, is the Hookio Battleground, site of a fierce battle between King Ka'akalaneo, of the Big Island of Hawaii and the Lanaians. King Ka'akalaneo, we are told, after suffering losses and defeat at the hands of King Kahekili of Maui, turned his wrath on Lanai, and in the battle that ensued, Ka'akalaneo's heavily armed warriors drove the Lanaians from the Hookio Gulch up the Hookio Ridge, where they eventually weakened from lack of food and water, and were then slaughtered or driven over the ridge to their deaths. The site of the battleground can be identified by looking down toward the Hookio Ridge, on the left of the trail — northward — and locating, at the crest of the ridge, three successive indentations — which, interestingly, are 20-foot wide, 8-foot-deep trenches, dug out and used by the Lanaians as their last defense.

Farther still, another mile or so, is the 3,370-foot summit of Lanaihale, the highest peak on Lanai from where you can see, on clear days, nearly all the inhabited islands of Hawaii — Oahu, Molokai, Maui, Kahoolawe and Hawaii, the Big Island. From Lanaihale, too, you can view the 2,000-foot-deep Hauola Gulch, Lanai's deepest canyon, as it winds toward the ocean.

The Munro Trail finally descends into the Palawai Basin, from where you can journey northwestward on the Hoike Road, a dirt trail, unmarked, which eventually merges with the Manele Road —Highway 440 — one and one-half miles south of Lanai City.

Palawai Basin

The Palawai Basin, encompassing some 6 square miles and lying just to the south of Lanai City, is essentially the crater of an extinct volcano that originally formed the island of Lanai. It was once also, quite interestingly, the site of a Mormon colony, appropriately named the "City of Joseph," established in 1854. The colony, however, failed in 1857, but was attempted again, a few years later, in 1861, under the leadership of a particularly enterprising Mormon missionary named Walter Murray Gibson. Gibson, as it turned out, was a man on a mission of his own. Over the years following the establishment of the colony, he purchased large tracts of land, supposedly for the Mormon Church, but systematically registering all the titles in his name; until, by 1875, he controlled fully 90% of all the land on Lanai, devoting much of it to goat and sheep ranching. Needless to say, the Mormon Church excommunicated Mr. Gibson forthwith, and the Mormon colony failed for the last time.

At any rate, the Palawai Basin now has in it, of interest to the visitor, the Luahiwa Petroglyphs — quite possibly the best preserved petroglyphs in the islands — reached by way of Manele Road — Highway 440 — south from Lanai City, one and one-half miles, then left — southeast — on Hoike Road, an unmarked dirt road that journeys through pineapple fields. From Hoike Road, a mile or so from the Manele Road turnoff, a dirt trail heads off northward, roughly three quarters of a mile, to the petroglyphs, found on several boulders scattered on a hillside, beneath some trees. The Luahiwa Petroglyphs, typically, feature symbols and stick figures representing humans, animals and birds, quite possibly dating from the late 1700s or early 1800s. The practice of making petroglyphs, of course, dates from the time of the first arrivals in Hawaii, and consists of etchings or carvings on rocks, made by either a blunt or a sharp, pointed tool, featuring symbols and stick figures of humans and animals — frequently thought to represent supernatural beings or gods — depicting scenes from daily life, such as hunting or dancing scenes. Much of the activity, it is believed, occured just prior to the arrival of Captain Cook in the islands in 1778, and continued until the 1860s.

Shipwreck Beach

Shipwreck Beach is the name given to the 8-mile stretch of coastline along the island's remote north coast, just off shore from where, on the reef in the Kalohi Channel, several ships have run aground over the years — hence the notoriety, and the name. Shipwreck Beach, however, comprises four or five smaller beaches — Awalua, Lapaiki, Po'aiwa, Federation Camp — all quite secluded, and with narrow strips of sand, backed by shallow sand dunes. The beaches, typically, offer some beachcombing and shoreline fishing possibilities, but swimming and snorkeling are not encouraged, largely due to the choppy seas.

In any case, Shipwreck Beach can be reached by way of Keomuku Road — Highway 430 — north from Lanai City, some 6½ miles, to the very bottom, where the paved road finally ends; then west on a rugged coastal road, a mile or so, to Federation Camp — a beach area used primarily by members of the Filipino Federation of America, a religious, cultural and social organization — and Po'aiwa, the last relatively easily accessible point on Shipwreck Beach. At Po'aiwa, however, you can search out the ruins of an old lighthouse, just to the north of the parking area, and also see a shipwreck just offshore from there — one of only two visible along the coast here

— believed to be that of a concrete-mud barge, run aground in 1960. Also from here, a marked trail, following painted rocks, leads inland a little way to some well-preserved petroglyphs, depicting human figures, dogs, centipedes, and hunting scenes.

Westward from Po'aiwa, of course, lie Lapaika and Awalua, 5 miles and 7 miles, respectively, reached on a wild sort of coastal trail, accessible, for the most part, on foot. Both beaches offer some fishing possibilities, but little else; and from Awalua you can see the second of the two visible shipwrecks along the coast here, just off shore, reportedly that of an old oil tanker, dating from the 1950s. Alawua and Lapaika, by the way, can also be reached by way of steep, rugged trails leading down from Polihua Road — which leads northwestward from Lanai City to the Garden of the Gods.

The East Coast

The east coast of Lanai is comprised primarily of Keomuku Beach — a 6-mile coastal stretch, extending from Kahokunui southeast to Halepalaoa — and south from Keomuku Beach to Lopa and Naha, two ancient fishing villages. The east coast of Lanai also, we might add, specifically the site of Lae Hi — unmarked, and difficult to locate — has its associations with Prince Kaululaau, son of Maui's King Kaakalaneo, who, in the 1400s, according to local lore, was banished to Lanai — an island inhabited solely by evil spirits at the time — as punishment for his incessant, mischievous behavior. Kaululaau, as the story goes, was left ashore here, on Lanai's east coast, and, mischievous as he was, he eluded the island's evil spirits by sleeping in a secret cave by the sea at night, while the spirits searched for him in vain. The spirits finally concluded that the young prince slept in the surf in the ocean, where, when they eventually looked for him, they drowned. Thus were the evil spirits of Lanai vanquished from the island, making it safe for habitation by humans, and Prince Kaululaau, as one would expect, returned to Maui a hero.

In any case, Keomuku Beach, quite like the adjacent Shipwreck Beach, can be reached more or less directly on Keomuku Road — Highway 430 — some $6\frac{1}{2}$ miles north from Lanai City. At the north end of Keomuku Road, where the paved portion of the road ends, sits Kahokunui, at the head of Keomuku Beach; and southeast from there, along a wild and bumpy dirt road, journeying along the coast, roughly $5\frac{1}{2}$ miles, lies Keomuku, site of the failed Maunalei sugar plantation. It was here, in 1898, that Walter Gibson's daughter, Talula, and her husband, Frederick Hayselden, attempted to establish a sugar plantation, forming the Maunalei Sugar Company. A pier was constructed at Halepalaoa Landing, just south of Keomuku, and in the process of building a railroad from Keomuku to Halepalaoa, the company, in order to obtain stones for laying the tracks, blasted part of the nearby Kahe'a Heiau — which can still be seen, in its dismantled state, just inland from Keomuku Road, a mile or so south of Keomuku. It was this act, however, of desecrating a sacred *heiau*, according to popular belief, that signalled the beginning of the end of the Maunalei company. In a matter of days, following the partial destruction of the heiau, the water for the mill, at its very source, turned brackish, and the plantation failed not long after, in 1900, when the company's Japanese labor force died of the plague that swept through the islands that year. Remnants of an old, abandoned locomotive can still be seen here, just inland from the main road, a little over a mile and a half south of Keomuku, reached by way of a short walk; and a little farther to the south, situated alongside the road itself, is a Japanese cemetery, where the Japanese laborers from the Maunalei company, who died of the plague, are buried.

At Keomuku itself, you can see some sites of the plantation town's homes, now overgrown with weeds. Here, too, amid a grove of coconut palms, is the old, ramshackle Ka Lanakila O Ka Mala-malama Church, the last structure to be left standing in Keomuku, originally built in 1903, and claimed to be the oldest church on the island. Also worth investigating, just to the north and south of Keomuku, respectively, on the *makai* side of the road, are the ruins of the ancient Ka'a and Wai'opae fishponds, visible at low tide.

Farther still, some 4 miles south of Keomuku — 2 miles south of Halepalaoa and the Japanese cemetery — lies Lopa, which has a small, sandy beach, with one or two picnic tables. Lopa also has in it an ancient fishpond, the remnants of which can be seen just to the south of the beach, beneath some palms.

Another 3 miles, south from Lopa, and we are at Naha, where the Keomuku Road finally ends. Naha is a former fishing village, which, however, is still frequented primarily by fishermen. It has, neverthe-less, a fishpond of interest, and an ancient paved trail, accessed only on foot, that leads from Naha to the Palawai Basin. The trailhead lies just to the south of the end of Keomuku Road, reached by crossing over a dry river bed and following a shoreline trail a short distance to the old paved trail, that dashes off inland. There are also some good views, a little way along the trail from the trailhead, of the islands of Maui and Kahoolawe.

Garden of the Gods

The "Garden of the Gods," many will tell you, is one of Lanai's hidden gems, especially interesting to geology buffs, located in the remote, rugged northern part of the island, and reached by way of Fraser Street directly northwest from Lanai City, passing through pineapple fields just on the outskirts of town, a little way, then Polihua Road, a dirt road, also northwestward, nearly 6 miles, to the unusual, eerie landscape of the Garden of the Gods.

The Garden of the Gods is indeed a strange natural phenomenon, where, in an eroded canyon of red soil, scores of boulders of various shapes, sizes and colors — in hues of red, blue and orange — lie scattered about, creating a lunar landscape of sorts. At sunset, the colors in the landscape are especially vibrant, well worth photo-graphing. There are also good views of the ocean from here.

From the Garden of the Gods, too, for the hardy souls, a rugged trail leads down to the remote, secluded Polihua Beach, some 4½ miles distant, with the last half mile or so accessible only on foot. Polihua — meaning "eggs in the bosom," and named for the fact that it was once a favorite nesting place for green sea turtles — is a beautiful, white-sand beach, rarely visited, and with great views of Molokai across the Kalohi Channel. It is, however, we must point out, also rather windy, and unsafe for swimming due to the strong ocean currents.

Finally, there is the Ka'ena Heiau, the largest *heiau* on the island, approximately 55 feet wide and 150 feet long, situated on a bluff overlooking the ocean, some 4 or 5 miles northwest of the Garden of the Gods. The *heiau* can be reached by way of the Polihua Trail, a mile from the Garden of the Gods, then the Ka'ena Trail that branches to the left, off the Polihua Trail, with the last 3 miles or so virtually impassable, leaving it only to the sure-footed and iron-willed to make the pilgrimage.

In any event, from the Garden of the Gods, you must retrace your route, on Polihua Road, back to Lanai City.

PRACTICAL INFORMATION FOR LANAI

HOW TO GET THERE

Lanai is situated approximately equidistant — 9 miles — from Maui and Molokai, which lie to its east and north, respectively. It can be reached by ferry from Maui, or on inter-island flights from Maui, Molokai or Oahu. Commercial flights arrive and depart at the island's main airport, the *Lanai Airport*, located near the southwest end of the island, some 3 miles from Lanai City; while ferries ply between Lahaina, Maui, and Lanai's *Manele Bay*.

By Air

Direct flights to Lanai from Maui, Molokai and Oahu are available on the following airlines: *Air Molokai* (808) 877-0026; *Aloha Airlines* (808) 244-9071; *Aloha IslandAir* (800) 652-6541; and *Hawaiian Airlines* (808) 882-8811. For schedules and fare information, contact the respective airlines. (Also see *How To Get There* in the *Maui* section for flights from the U.S. mainland to Maui and Honolulu, Oahu.)

By Ferry

Ferry services are available daily between Manele Bay, Lanai, and Lahaina, Maui. The one-way adult fare is $25.00. For departure and arrival times and more information, contact *Expeditions on Maui*, P.O. Box 1763, Lahaina, HI 96767; (808) 661-3756.

TOURIST INFORMATION

Hawaii Visitors Bureau (HVB). Waikiki Business Plaza, 2270 Kalakaua Ave., Suite 808, Honolulu, HI 96815. Offers a wealth of tourist information, including directory of accommodations and restaurants and a calendar of events. Also maps, and a tourist publication, *The Islands of Hawaii: A Vacation Planner*, covering places of interest on the islands, recreation and tours. The *Hawaii Visitors Bureau* also maintains an office on Maui, for visitors arriving on Lanai from Maui; *Maui Visitors Bureau*, 250 Alamaha St., Kahului, HI 96733; (808) 871-8691.

HOW TO GET AROUND

By Car. Rental cars are available from two different car rental agencies, both located in Lanai City. Rental rates for sub-compacts to larger luxury cars range from $18-$70 per day to $180-$320 per week. Both companies also offer four-wheel-drive vehicles, especially useful if you plan to visit some of the more remote parts of the island; rental rates for four-wheel-drives is usually around $100 per day. For rentals, availability and more information, contact either *Dollar*, 1036 Lanai Ave., Lanai City, (808) 565-7227/(800) 342-7398; or *AA Paradise Network*, (800) 942-2242.

ACCOMMODATIONS

Hotel Lanai. *$65-$75.* 828 Lanai Ave., Lanai City; (808) 565-7211. 10 units. Restaurant and cocktail lounge on premises.

The Lodge at Koele. *$295-$975.* Keomuku Hwy. (44), Lanai City; (808) 565-7300/(800) 321-4666. 102-unit luxury hotel. Room phones, swimming pool, tennis court, golf course, stables, restaurants and cocktail lounge, and meeting rooms.

The Manele Bay Hotel. *$225-$595.* Manele Bay Rd. (440), Manele Bay; (808) 565-7700/(800) 321-4666. 250 rooms and suites in oceanfront resort hotel. Room phones and air-conditioning; also swimming pool, health club and spa, golf course, tennis courts, restaurants and cocktail lounge, meeting rooms, and beauty salon.

PLACES OF INTEREST

Garden of the Gods. Located in the remote, rugged northern part of the island, and reached by way of Fraser St. northwest from Lanai City to the outskirts of town, then Polihua Rd., a dirt road, another 6 miles northwestward to the Garden of the Gods. This is one of the island's foremost attractions, where, in an eroded canyon of red soil, scores of boulders of various shapes, sizes and colors — in hues of red, blue and orange, especially vibrant at sunset — lie scattered about, creating a lunar landscape of sorts. There are also good views of the ocean from here.

Hulopoe Beach. At the bottom end of Hwy. 440 (Manele Rd.), approximately 7 miles south of Lanai City. Crescent-shaped white-sand beach, one of Hawaii's loveliest beaches, situated at the head of Hulopoe Bay. Offers some of the best snorkeling and diving in the islands, with abundant marine life and coral, all protected as part of the Manele-Hulopoe Marine Life Conservatory District. Also safe swimming conditions, including a nearby natural rock wading pool for children, and picnic tables, barbecue pits, and volleyball courts.

Kaunolu. Located in the southwest corner of the island, nearly 8 miles from Lanai City, and reached by way of Manele Rd. (440) south from Lanai City some 4 miles, then westward onto Kaupili Rd., a rugged dirt road, another 2½ miles, from where the wild Kaunolu Rd. dashes off toward the ocean, another 3 miles or so — making a sharp left just three-quarter mile from the Kaupili Rd. turnoff and a sharp right a quarter mile farther — along an especially bumpy descent, to Kaunolu. Kaunolu itself is the site of an ancient fishing village, which was once the favorite vacation retreat of Kamehameha I, and which still has in it the sites of some 86 houses and 35 shelters — one of the best preserved ruins in the Hawaiian islands. There is also a large heiau here, the Halulu Heiau, together with some petroglyphs, and Kahekili's Leap, with its sheer, 90-foot drop to the ocean below.

The Luahiwa Petroglyphs. Located in the Palawai Basin, more or less in the center of the island; reached by way of Manele Rd. (440) south from Lanai City, approximately 1½ miles (just past mile marker 7), then left — southeast — on Hoike Rd., an unmarked dirt road, another mile or so, and off on a dirt trail (which goes off Hoike Rd.), northward, roughly three quarters of a mile, to the petroglyphs. The Luahiwa Petroglyphs are among the best preserved petroglyphs in the islands, quite possibly dating from the late 1700s and early 1800s, and featuring symbols and stick figures representing humans, animals and birds.

Munro Trail. 8-mile trail, just to the east of Lanai City. The trailhead is located northeast of Lanai City, a mile past the Lodge at Koele, with the sign-posted trail heading off eastward from Keomuku Rd. (Hwy. 44), winding through groves of Norfolk Island pine and a lush, tropical rain forest, passing over the Lanaihale ridge, the highest point in Lanai, at an elevation of 3,370 feet, with views of the 2,000-foot-deep Hauola Gulch, the Maunalei and Wahane gulches, and, on clear days, the islands of Oahu, Molokai, Maui, Kaho'olawe and Hawaii. The trail is accessible only in a four-wheel-drive vehicle, or on foot.

Shipwreck Beach. Situated along the island's remote north coast, and reached on Keomuku Rd. (Hwy. 430) north from Lanai City, some 6½ miles, to the very end, then west on a rugged, coastal, dirt road, another mile or so, to the start of the beach. The beach comprises approximately 8 miles of shoreline, including a series of smaller beach areas — Federation Camp,

Po'aiwa, Lapaika and Awalua — all quite secluded, and with narrow strips of sand, backed by shallow sand dunes. The beaches offer some beach-combing and shoreline fishing possibilities, but swimming and snorkeling are not encouraged, due to the choppy seas. There are also two shipwrecks visible just offshore from the beach — one of a concrete-mud barge, run aground in 1960; and another of an old oil tanker, dating from the 1950s.

Keomuku. Situated on the east coast of the island, east of Lanai City, and reached by way of Keomuku Rd. (Hwy. 430) north from Lanai City, $6\frac{1}{2}$ miles, to the very end, then southeast along the coast another $5\frac{1}{2}$ miles, on a bumpy dirt road, to Keomuku. Keomuku itself is the site of the failed, late 19th-century Maunalei sugar plantation, where the sites of some old plantation homes are still visible, as well as the old ramshackle Ka Lanakila O Ka Malamalama Church, the last structure to be left standing in Keomuku, dating from 1903 and with the distinction of being the oldest church on the island, nestled in a grove of coconut palms.

GOLF COURSES

The Experience at Koele. Keomuku Rd. (44), Lanai City; (808) 565-4653. 18-hole, championship course, at an elevation of 1,600 feet, designed by Greg Norman; 7,102 yards, par 72. Green fees: $95.00-$140.00 (including cart). Pro shop, driving range, and club rentals.

The Challenge at Manele Bay. Manele Bay; (808) 565-3800. 18-hole, Jack Nicklaus-designed championship course; 7,000-7,600 yards, par 72. Green fees: $99.00 for guests of Manele Bay Hotel, $140.00 for non-guests. Pro shop, driving range, club rentals.

TENNIS

Facilities for tennis are available at the following locations on the island: *Lodge at Koele,* Keomuku Rd. (Hwy.44), Lanai City, (808) 565-7300; and *Manele Bay Hotel,* Manele Bay Rd. (440), Manele Bay, (808) 565-7700/(800) 321-4666. The *Lodge at Koele* facility has 3 courts, with no lights, and the *Manele Bay* facility has 6 courts, also with no lights. Both facilities are open to the public, available to hotel guests at no cost, and to non-guests, at a fee of around $10.00 per day.

RESTAURANTS

(Restaurant prices — based on full-course dinner, excluding drinks, tax and tips — are categorized as follows; *Deluxe,* over $30; *Expensive,* $20-$30; *Moderate,* $10-$20; *Inexpensive,* under $10.)

Blue Ginger Cafe. *Inexpensive.* 409 7th Ave., Lanai City; (808) 565-6363. Standard breakfast fare, including freshly-baked pastries, and plate lunches. Open for breakfast and lunch Mon.-Sat.

Hotel Lanai. *Inexpensive-Moderate.* 828 Lanai Ave., Lanai City; (808) 565-7211. Serves hearty breakfasts, and lunches and dinners featuring fresh fish, pasta, steaks and poultry, and a salad bar. Open daily.

Hulopoe Court. *Moderate-Expensive.* At the Manele Bay Hotel, Manele Rd. (440), Manele Bay; (808) 565-7700. Features contemporary Hawaiian regional cuisine, served in a Mediterranean setting. Open for breakfast, lunch and dinner. Reservations suggested.

Ihi Lani. *Expensive-Deluxe.* At the Manele Bay Hotel, Manele Rd. (440), Manele Bay; (808) 565-7700. Well-appointed restaurant, in open-air setting, overlooking Hulopoe Bay. Serves gourmet French-Mediterranean cuisine. Open for dinner daily. Reservations recommended.

The Lodge at Koele. *Deluxe.* At The Lodge at Koele, Keomuku Rd. (44), Lanai City; (808) 565-7300. Elegant, well-appointed restaurant, specializing in French cuisine. Menu features fresh fish, lobster, steak, and axis deer. Open for dinner. Reservations recommended.

The Pool Grille. *Moderate.* Manele Bay Hotel, Manele Rd., Manele Bay; (808) 565-7700. Casual poolside restaurant, serving primarily sandwiches, salads and grilled entrees. Open for lunch daily.

S.T. Properties. *Inexpensive.* 419 7th Ave., Lanai City; (808) 565-6537. Popular local eatery. Offers home-style breakfast, plate lunches, and burgers. Open for breakfast and lunch daily.

The Terrace. *Expensive.* At the Lodge at Koele, Keomuku Rd. (44), Lanai City; (808) 565-7300. Casual setting; overlooking beautiful gardens and a reflection pond. Offers contemporary Hawaiian cuisine, with emphasis on fresh fish, steak and lobster. Breakfast, lunch and dinner daily. Reservations suggested.

HAWAIIAN GLOSSARY

The Hawaiian language, in its simplicity, contains only seven consonants — H, K, L, M, N, P, W — and five vowels — A, E, I, O and U. All words — and syllables — end in a vowel, and all syllables begin with a consonant. The vowels, typically, are each pronounced separately — i.e., *a'a* is pronounced "ah-ah," and *e'e* is pronounced "ay-ay"; the only exceptions are the diphthong double vowels — *ai*, pronounced "eye," and *au*, pronounced "ow." The consonants, on the other hand, are never doubled.

Hawaiian consonants are pronounced similar to those in English, with the notable exception of W, which is sometimes pronounced as "V," when it begins the last syllable of the word. Hawaiian vowels are pronounced as follows: A - "uh," as in among; E - "ay," as in day; I - "ee," as in deep; O - "oh," as in no; U - "oo," as in blue.

For travellers to the Hawaiian islands, the following is a glossary of some commonly used words in the Hawaiian language.

a'a — rough, crumbling lava.

ae — yes.

ahi — tuna fish.

ahupua'a — pie-shaped land division, extending from the mountains to the sea.

aikane — friend.

alanui — road, or path.

ali'i — a Hawaiian chief or nobleman.

aloha — love, or affection; traditional Hawaiian greeting, meaning both welcome and farewell.

anu — cold, cool.

a'ole — no.

auwe — alas!

awawa — valley.

hala — the pandanus tree, the leaves of which are used to make baskets and mats.

hale — house.

hale pule — church; house of worship.

hana — work.

hahana — hot, warm.

haole — foreigner; frequently used to refer to a Caucasian.

hapa — half, as in *hapa-haole*, or half Caucasian.

haupia — coconut cream pudding, often served at a luau.

heiau — an ancient Hawaiian place of worship; shrine, temple.

holoholo — to go for a walk; also to ride or sail.

honi — a kiss; also, to kiss.

hui — a group, society, or assembly of people.

hukilau — a communal fishing party, in which everyone helps pull in the fishing nets.

hula — traditional Hawaiian dance of storytelling.
imu — underground oven, used for roasting pigs for luaus.
ipo — sweetheart, or lover.

ka'ahele — a tour.
ka'ao — legend.
kahuna — priest, minister, sorcerer, prophet.
kai — the sea.
kakahiaka — morning.
kama'aina — native-born, or local.
kanaka — man, usually of Hawaiian descent.
kane — male, husband.
kapu — taboo, forbidden; derived from the Tongan word, *tabu*.
keiki — child; a male child is known as *keikikane*, and a female child, *keikiwahine*.
kiawe — Algaroba tree, with fern-like leaves and sharp, long thorns, usually found in dry areas near the coast. Kiawe wood is used to make charcoal for fuel. The tree was introduced to Hawaii in the 1820s.
koa — native Hawaiian tree, prized for its wood which was used by early Hawaiians to craft canoes, spears and surfboards. Koa wood is now used to make fine furniture.
kokua — help.
kona — leeward side of island; frequently used to describe storms and winds, such as *kona* storm or *kona* wind. Also, south.
ko'olau — windward side of island.
kukui — Candlenut tree, characteristic in its yellow and green foliage, generally found in the valleys. Kukui nuts are also used in leis. Kukui is Hawaii's state tree.
kuleana — home site, or homestead; also responsibility, or one's business.
kupuna — grandparent.

lamalama — torch fishing
lanai — porch, veranda, balcony.
lani — the sky, or heaven
laulau — wrapped package; generally used to describe bundles of pork, fish or beef, served with taro shoots, wrapped in *ti* or banana leaves, and steamed.
lei — garland, wreath, or necklace of flowers.
lilikoi — passion fruit.
limu — seaweed.
luau — traditional Hawaiian feast.

mahalo — thanks, or thank you.
mahimahi — dolphin.
maile — native vine with shiny, fragrant leaves used in leis.
makahiki hou — New Year; *hauoli makahiki hou*, Happy New Year.
make — to die, or dead.

makai — toward the ocean, or seaward.
malihini — stranger, newcomer.
mana — supernatural power.
manu — bird.
mauka — toward the mountain, or inland.
mauna — mountain.
mele — song, chant.
menehune — Hawaii's legendary little people, ingenious and hardworking, who worked only at night, building fishponds, heiaus, irrigation ditches and roads, many of which remain today.
moana — the ocean; open sea.
mo'o — lizard, dragon, serpent.
mu'umu'u — long, loose, traditional Hawaiian dress.

nani — beautiful.
nui — big.

ohana — family.
ono — delicious.

pakalolo — marijuana.
palapala — book; also printing.
pali — cliff; also plural, cliffs.
paniolo — Hawaiian cowboy.
pau — finished, all done.
poi — a purplish paste made from pounded and cooked taro roots; staple of Hawaiian diet.
puka — hole, opening.
pupu — appetizer, snack, hors d'oeuvre.
pupule — crazy; insane.

tapa — cloth made from beaten bark, often used in Hawaiian clothing.
taro — broad-leafed plant with starch root, used to make poi; staff of life of early Hawaiians, introduced to the islands by the first Polynesians.
ti — broad-leafed plant, brought to Hawaii by early Polynesian immigrants. *Ti* leaves are used for wrapping food as well as offerings to the gods.

waha — mouth; *waha nui*, a big mouth.
wahine — female, woman, wife.
wai — fresh water.
wiki — to hurry; *wikiwiki*, hurry up.

HAWAIIAN FLOWERS

Hibiscus

Anthurium

Bird of Paradise

Torch Ginger

White Ginger

136

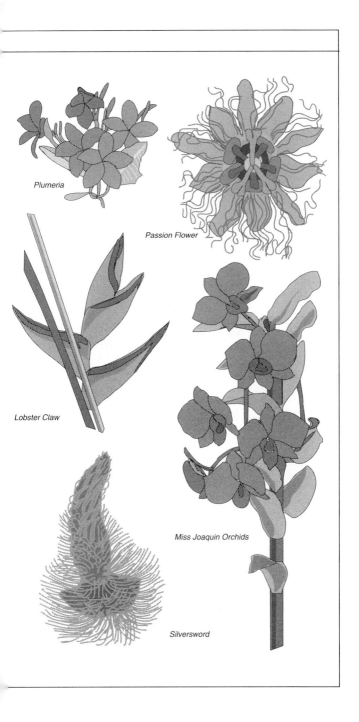

Plumeria

Passion Flower

Lobster Claw

Miss Joaquin Orchids

Silversword

137

HAWAIIAN REEF FISH

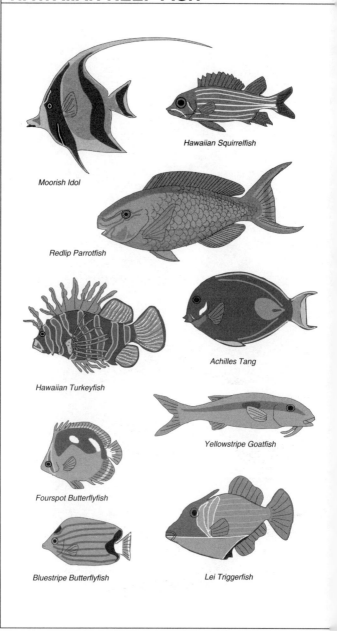

Moorish Idol

Hawaiian Squirrelfish

Redlip Parrotfish

Hawaiian Turkeyfish

Achilles Tang

Fourspot Butterflyfish

Yellowstripe Goatfish

Bluestripe Butterflyfish

Lei Triggerfish

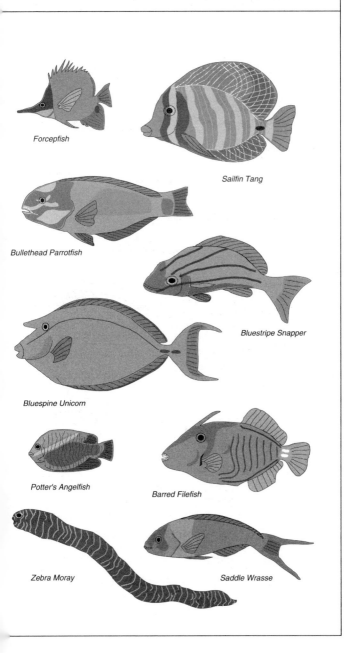

Forcepfish

Sailfin Tang

Bullethead Parrotfish

Bluestripe Snapper

Bluespine Unicorn

Potter's Angelfish

Barred Filefish

Zebra Moray

Saddle Wrasse

INDEX

The abbreviation MA stands for Maui.
The abbreviation MO stands for Molokai.
The abbreviation LA stands for Lanai